ISSN 0265-4105

BRITISH RAILWAY JOURNAL

CONTENTS

Edited and designed by Paul Karau.

WILD SWAN PUBLICATIONS LTD.,
1-3 Hagbourne Road, Didcot, Oxon, OX11 8DP.
Telephone: Didcot (01235) 816478.

Subscriptions: 2 issues – £19.90 post free (U.K. only). Overseas rates on application. Cheques should be made payable to 'Wild Swan Publications Ltd.' and sent to the above address.

Articles and advertisements should be sent to:
British Railway Journal, Wild Swan Publications Ltd.,
1-3 Hagbourne Road, Didcot, Oxon, OX11 8DP.
Telephone Didcot (01235) 816478 during office hours

Please include SAE with all articles and illustrations submitted for return in case of non-acceptance.

Authors must have permission to reproduce all photographs, drawings, etc., submitted.

Whilst every care is taken, the publishers cannot accept responsibility for the actions of any advertisers in the magazine.

Printed by Amadeus Press, Cleckheaton, West Yorkshire.

EDITORIAL

Railways may be a minority interest, but those of us with a passion for the steam railway system as it was are remarkably lucky that continuing activity by historians, photograph collectors, preservationists, modellers, etc., have kept the scene alive in a variety of ways. Detailed accounts or even the briefest feature in periodicals continue to fuel our interest and understanding of the past.

I grew up without doubting that when I was old enough I would be able to enjoy and explore the railways that I experienced on family train journeys. No one in my family was interested in railways, so I never expected them to understand the excitement that stirred from the back seat on a car journey when I spotted a railway bridge or level crossing, even if there were no trains in view.

As I grew older and ever more eager, a number of the branch lines I wanted to visit were closed, steam disappeared quite soon in our area and the general infrastructure began to change. It seemed it was all over. Who could have imagined that over fifty years later we would all be awaiting the latest railway history or discovering new pictures in the variety of magazines on the newsagents' shelves? Who would have thought we could have enjoyed today's preserved lines where we could sit in pre-nationalisation carriages hauled by steam and experience all the associated smuts and odours? With the passage of time, some locomotives have been longer in preservation service than on British Railways.

As the years pass, the remains of abandoned railways naturally become less obvious with urban development, road schemes, landfill and, more naturally, young saplings that took root in the ballast and have grown into trees, emphasising how long ago it all passed.

Because the Brill Tramway closed in 1935, it seemed all the more remote to me and that probably heightened its romantic appeal. Thankfully, one of the Metropolitan A Class 4–4–0Ts, No. 23, survives in the London Transport Museum but its showcase (and cabless) condition doesn't make it quite so easy to relate to pictures of it running across Buckinghamshire pastures.

I have always wanted to be able to visualize the whole of this rustic byway and imagine what it must have been like to journey out to Brill, but collecting suitable photographs over the years has been more a matter of chance. Thankfully, our good friend Roger Carpenter had a similar interest and has very kindly allowed me to fill in some of the gaps from his own collection. We still haven't managed to track down a gradient profile for the route and, as far as we can tell, the only surviving record is the mention of the gradients in a Board of Trade inspection report.

So, 75 years after the end of the Brill Tramway, we are at last able to illustrate the route. I would still like to fill in gaps in the coverage, but even as it stands, this record has devoured more pages than anticipated, so we only get as far as Wotton in this issue!

Paul Karau

Aldeburgh station, looking north and probably photographed in the early 1900s when it was still very much in its original condition.

THE ALDEBURGH BRANCH

By STANLEY C. JENKINS and CHRIS TURNER

Situated in a remote and exposed position on the lonely east Suffolk coast, the quaint old borough of Aldeburgh was once a place of considerable importance. In Tudor times its sprat and herring fisheries employed over 1,000 fishermen, while from 1571 until 1832 the town returned two members of Parliament.

Unfortunately, this thriving and prosperous fishing port was built on a notoriously impermanent stretch of coast, and in later years many of its streets and houses were overwhelmed by the encroaching sea. Indeed, in the 18th Century there were fears that the entire town would be destroyed without trace, but in the event the fickle sea threw up a protective ridge of shingle, behind which the surviving parts of the town were able to obtain at least some shelter in the years to come.

By early Victorian times Aldeburgh was a picturesque, but somewhat decayed backwater. The population in 1851 was only 1,627 and fishing remained the principal economic activity, sprats and herring being the usual catches.

On the face of it, this remote Suffolk fishing settlement was hardly the sort of place to which Victorian capitalists would have rushed to build a railway, and in fact the Aldeburgh branch, as finally built, *was* very much an afterthought – Leiston, rather than Aldeburgh, being the main objective of the railway builders.

ORIGINS OF THE BRANCH

Railway development in the Aldeburgh area commenced during the Railway Mania years of the 1840s, when local entrepreneurs promoted a scheme which, if implemented, would have linked Ipswich, Woodbridge, Halesworth and Bungay. This initial scheme was not immediately successful, but on 5th June 1851 the Halesworth, Beccles & Haddiscoe Railway was incorporated by Act of Parliament (14 Vic. cap.26) with powers to build a line southwards from Haddiscoe on the Reedham to Lowestoft line of the Lowestoft Railway & Harbour Company.

The Haddiscoe to Halesworth line was opened on 4th December 1854, by which time the original company had changed its name to 'The East Suffolk Railway' and obtained further powers by an Act passed

on 3rd July 1854 for an extension to Woodbridge, where an end-on junction would be made with the projected Ipswich to Woodbridge line of the Eastern Union Railway. By this same Act (17 & 18 Vic. cap. 109) powers were also obtained for branches to Framlingham, Snape and Leiston, the combined length of the East Suffolk main line and its branches being 53 miles.

Two local companies, the Lowestoft & Beccles Railway and the Yarmouth & Haddiscoe Railway, were incorporated into the East Suffolk company by an Act of 23rd July 1858, and the ESR was opened throughout from Yarmouth and Lowestoft to Ipswich on 1st June 1859. Although nominally an independent concern, the East Suffolk Railway was leased to its contractor Sir Morton Peto (1809-1889), and worked under an operating agreement with the Eastern Counties Railway.

The newly-opened railway provided a useful diversionary route for traffic between Norwich, Yarmouth, Lowestoft and Ipswich while, for local farmers and traders, it also provided much-needed transport facilities for small towns and villages such as Halesworth, Darsham and Saxmundham. There were, in addition to the ESR main line, the branch lines to Leiston, Framlingham and Snape, the latter being a freight-only route; all of these lines were opened simultaneously with the main line on 1st June 1859.

The Leiston branch diverged from the ESR main line at Saxmundham Junction and ran eastwards across easy terrain for slightly less than four miles, albeit with an initial stretch of 1 in 58 rising gradient, followed by a gentle 1 in 121 descent for a further mile. At its eastern end the newly-opened railway terminated at Leiston in convenient proximity to Richard Garrett's

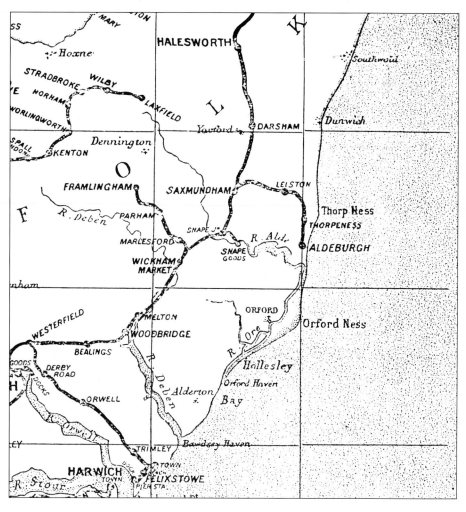

well-known agricultural engineering works, which had been established in 1778.

It was envisaged that Garrett's works would generate profitable industrial traffic for the East Suffolk line, with coal flowing inwards to Leiston and finished vehicles and machinery being dispatched by train; significantly, a later Richard Garrett was a director of the East Suffolk company, his presence on the board serving to underline the close links between Garretts and the railway.

In common with the rest of the East Suffolk system, the Leiston branch was worked from its inception by the Eastern Counties Railway. The original passenger timetable dated 1st June 1859 provided a modest service of four trains in each direction, with up trains from Leiston at 6.40 am, 11.45 am, 4.25 pm and 7.00 pm. In the down direction, the balancing eastbound workings left Saxmundham at 8.05 am, 1.15 pm, 3.30 pm and 7.55 pm. The 6.40 am up service and the 1.15 pm down workings were the statutory 'Parliamentary' trains which conveyed low-income travellers at the rate of just one (old) penny per mile, as well as first, second and third class passengers. The Sunday service consisted of two trains in each direction.

The advertised fares from Leiston to London were 19s. 8d. first class, 15s. 9d. second class, 11s.10d. third class and 7s. 10½d. for Parliamentary class travellers.

EXTENSION TO ALDEBURGH

Having obtained powers for the branch to Leiston, the East Suffolk directors were amenable to local suggestions that the original line could easily be extended southwards to Aldeburgh, a distance of about four miles. With no physical obstacles en route, it was hoped that the extension could be built relatively cheaply. A Bill was therefore prepared for submission to Parliament in the 1859 session, and this new proposal received the Royal Assent on 19th April 1859.

The resulting Act (22 Vic. cap. 28) authorised the construction of a 4 mile 32 chain railway commencing in Leiston by a junction with the branch from Saxmundham and terminating in Aldeburgh on the north-west side of the town. In conjunction with this scheme the East Suffolk company was permitted to raise a further £40,000 in ten pound shares and £13,333 by loan, the estimated cost of the new line being £40,000. A period of two years was allowed for the compulsory pur-

chase of land, and three years was allowed for completion of the works.

Having obtained Parliamentary consent for the Aldeburgh extension, the East Suffolk directors lost no time in putting their scheme into effect. The authorised route ran due east from Leiston for a short distance and then turned southwards across gently undulating terrain for the remainder of the way to Aldeburgh. It was reported that there were 'no peculiar engineering difficulties, and no tunnels'; the gradients and curves were generally favourable, the sharpest curve having a radius of 40 chains while the steepest gradient was said to be no more than 1 in 82.6.

The railway builders made rapid progress, and the Aldeburgh line was opened for traffic on 12th April 1860, just one year after the passing of the Act authorising its construction.

The completed branch from Saxmundham to Aldeburgh was single track throughout with an intermediate station at Leiston. The line was worked by the Eastern Counties Railway, the necessary locomotives, rolling stock and staff being provided by the ECR company under previously-agreed terms. There were no major bridges or large earthworks, but the $8\frac{3}{4}$ mile route passed over numerous level crossings. There was just one road underbridge, this modest structure being situated near Leiston.

UNDER GREAT EASTERN CONTROL

As we have seen, the East Suffolk system and its connections had been built by a bewildering assortment of small, local companies, but most of these had fallen under Eastern Counties control by the early 1860s. In 1862 the process whereby the ECR acquired control of its smaller neighbours culminated in a long-overdue amalgamation, and on 7th August an Act (25 & 26 Vic. cap. 223) to 'Amalgamate the Eastern-Counties, the East Anglian, the Newmarket, the Eastern Union, and the Norfolk Railway companies' received the Royal Assent.

Although in effect the Eastern Counties company had merely absorbed lines that it already controlled, the company wisely decided to rename itself 'The Great Eastern Railway', thereby proclaiming a distinct break with the past and underlining the creation of a new, fully-unified railway system. As far as the East Suffolk network was concerned, the Great Eastern issued

£675,000 worth of debenture and preference stock to the ESR proprietors as part of a complex arrangement whereby the East Suffolk's debts and liabilities were indemnified.

As a result of this deal, the Aldeburgh branch, together with the rest of the former East Suffolk Railway, passed into Great Eastern control, and these local Suffolk lines thereby became part of an extensive East Anglian railway system.

TRAINS & TRAFFIC IN THE GREAT EASTERN ERA

Garrett's engineering works provided an important source of traffic for the line from its earliest years while, with a rail link to the outside world, Messrs Garrett were able to fully develop an extensive export trade. By the end of the 19th century 'Garretts of Leiston' were a household name in many parts of the world, the export of traction engines to Australia and other parts of the British Empire being a major aspect of the firm's activities. In fact, Garrett engines were probably better-known outside England than within it – Australian farmers are said to have much preferred Garrett engines to rival Fowler machines

Whilst local fisherman no doubt benefited from the new rail link, holiday traffic, as such, played a very minor role during the Victorian period. Few industrial workers took summer holidays in the 19th century, and although there is evidence that well-off middle class families spent their summers in 'watering places' such as Aldeburgh, the actual numbers involved would have been exceedingly small by the standards of later years.

In the case of Aldeburgh, the middle class invasion had started to take place before the coming of the railway, the provision of turnpike roads being an important factor in this context. The first edition of *White's History, Gazetteer & Directory of Suffolk* (1844) provides an interesting glimpse into what might be termed the origins of Aldeburgh's holiday trade:

'Till the commencement of the present century, Aldeburgh, impoverished, and depopulated by the encroachments of the ocean, was hastening to decay; but several families of distinction, wishing for a greater degree of privacy and retirement than can be enjoyed in a fashionable watering place, having made it their summer residence, its appearance has, since that period, been totally changed. The deep sands which formerly led to it have given place to excellent turnpike roads; and instead of the clay-built cottages, which gave the place a squalid appearance, are now seen neat and comfortable dwellings, and several large and handsome mansions, which are the occasional retreat of persons of rank and fortune.'

Clearly, these occasional summer residents would not in themselves have provided much traffic for the new railway, but the presence of 'persons of rank and fortune' was usually the first step towards the creation of larger and more fashionable resorts in hitherto remote seaside areas, and something of this nature took place at Aldeburgh. At the same time, the Great Eastern Railway was only too pleased to cater for growing numbers of summer visitors, and in an attempt to stimulate demand for travel to the coast, the company started issuing first, second and third class cheap tickets to Aldeburgh from London and intermediate stations, together with a range of first and second class two-monthly return tickets from London and principal GER stations, and first, second and third class weekly return tickets between London and Aldeburgh. In addition, the Great Eastern introduced second and third class day excursion tickets on Mondays to Aldeburgh from all East Suffolk line stations between Ipswich and Saxmundham, whilst the Midland, London & North Western and other companies advertised first and second class two-monthly return tickets from a variety of stations throughout the country.

This vigorous and enterprising policy did much to popularise Aldeburgh as a fashionable seaside resort, and in 1865 *Measom's Guide to the Great Eastern Railway* could confidently state that:

'The Great Eastern Railway branch line is rapidly improving the town, and from the salubrity of the air, and the convenience of the shore for sea-bathing, it has lately become a place of fashionable resort during the summer.'

In similar vein, the 1865 *Post Office Directory of Suffolk* noted that Aldeburgh was 'much resorted to in summer for bathing'; many 'pretty villas' had recently been erected on the sea front for letting as summer residences, and there were also 'two commodious hotels'.

The line was originally worked as one section between Saxmundham Junction and Aldeburgh, train staff and ticket operation being introduced on 1st October 1866. Before that date the branch had been worked under 'Rule 141' of the Eastern Counties Railway Rule Book (1854), which related to the operation of single-track railways without telegraphic communication. This meant that in practice the

The frontage of Saxmundham station, probably in the 1920s. The photographer was standing with his back to the town and facing west. The building gave access to the up side of the line.

Aldeburgh line was worked on the one-engine-in-steam system, with the proviso that a special train or light engine might be permitted to enter the single line if written notice had previously been sent to each station en route by a preceding train, and that an additional red tail light (by night) or a red tailboard (by day) was placed on the train preceding the special working.

Block telegraph operation was introduced on the line around 1891, though Leiston remained a non-staff station until World War One. The train staff in use at that time was round in section and green in colour.

The branch train service had increased to around half a dozen workings in each direction by the 1880s. The April 1882 timetable, for example, provided six up and six down services, with up trains from Aldeburgh at 7.02 am, 8.55 am, 12.00 pm, 2.25 pm, 4.25 pm and 6.55 pm, and corresponding down workings from Saxmundham at 8.10 am, 11.30 am, 12.45 pm, 3.05 pm, 5.25 pm and 7.45 pm. Average journey times were about 22 minutes for the 8¼ mile journey.

The summer service, which came into effect from July 1882, was generally similar, though the number of trains was increased to seven in each direction. In the up direction, trains left Aldeburgh at 7.05 am, 8.55 am, 12.30 pm, 1.45 pm, 3.00 pm, 4.35 pm and 6.55 pm, whilst the down workings left Saxmundham at 8.10 am, 11.30 am, 1.10 pm, 2.30 pm, 3.41 pm, 5.25 pm and 7.45 pm. The up services took 21 minutes, except for the 8.55 am which took only

20 minutes, and the 6.55 pm, which was allowed 30 minutes. The down workings accomplished their journeys in 22 minutes, apart from the 8.10 am departure from Aldeburgh, which reached Saxmundham in 25 minutes.

An innovation, from around 1905 onwards, was the introduction of a daily through portion from Aldeburgh to Liverpool Street, which was attached to an up Lowestoft express at Saxmundham and then ran non-stop to London. This service catered for long-distance commuters rather than holidaymakers, although the provision of through coaches to and from London was obviously a factor in the subsequent development of Aldeburgh as a small, but select holiday resort.

There were usually three down and four up through carriages daily during the summer months, with at least one through working during the winter period. The daily winter through train did not run non-stop between Saxmundham and Liverpool Street, but two of the four summer through workings ran non-stop from Saxmundham to London; these were the 2.01 pm from Aldeburgh (arr. Liverpool Street 4.33 pm) and the 4.22 pm from Aldeburgh (arr. Liverpool Street 6.53 pm). The other summer through trains to London were the 8.47 am and 12.27 pm services from Aldeburgh, which reached Liverpool Street at 11.35 am and 3.43 pm respectively. In the down direction, the three summer through trains left Liverpool Street at 10.27 am, 12.30 pm and 3.43 pm, whilst in the winter the single through working left Aldeburgh at 8.50 am and returned from Liverpool Street at 3.25 pm.

A further development, in terms of future holiday traffic on the Aldeburgh line, came on 29th July 1914, when the GER opened a small station at Thorpeness. In the longer term, this new stopping place encouraged the growth of a bungalow settlement on what had been open coastal land, though large scale development on the site did not really begin until the 1920s.

It is known that during the 1880s Massey Bromley's 'E10' class 0-4-4Ts worked the branch passenger services. On 30th August 1882 'E10' class 0-4-4T No.97 was derailed at Leiston while working a branch passenger train.

WORLD WAR ONE

The outbreak of war in 1914 was a catalyst which brought many changes. The GER and other main-line railway companies were placed under government control as part of the national war effort, train services being cut or otherwise amended to serve a wider strategic need. At Leiston, the Garrett works was pressed into service as a munitions factory, whilst Aldeburgh was chosen as the site of a Royal Naval Air Station.

Although railwaymen were exempt from general conscription when that measure was introduced in 1916, large numbers of men volunteered for active service, and this placed great strains on companies such as the GER, which was forced to employ large numbers of women and men who would otherwise have retired.

Many of those who had so willingly volunteered for military service lost their lives on the Western Front or elsewhere, and in this context the practice of placing men from the same streets or villages in a single unit (to foster team spirit) led to tragedy when those units were sent into action. Perhaps for this reason, Saxmundham station seems to have lost a disproportionately high number of former employees, including gate lad & porter William Leeder, gate lad Eric Edmunds and lad porter Samuel Copping, all of whom lost their lives between 1916 and 1918. Eric Edmund's father, (who also worked for the Great Eastern as a Gate Keeper at Saxmundham) was so affected by the loss of his son that he became an active charity worker, devoting much of his time to money-raising activities on behalf of prisoners-of-war and the East Suffolk & Ipswich Hospital.

A special occasion at Leiston with an exceptional crowd of Edwardian excursionists waiting to board the approaching train.

An unidentified Y14 0-6-0 tender engine at Leiston station in Great Eastern Railway days, probably working on the branch goods. The class were first built in 1883 and under the LNER were classified as J15.

For operational purposes, the branch was divided into two, single-line train staff sections between December 1914 and July 1915, the sections being Saxmundham Junction to Leiston and Leiston to Aldeburgh; the Saxmundham Junction to Leiston train staff was now round in section and green in colour, whilst the Leiston to Aldeburgh train staff was square in section and red in colour. Through coaches continued to run throughout the 1914–18 war, with one train in each direction conveying through vehicles between Liverpool Street and Aldeburgh.

In common with other east coast areas, the Aldeburgh region found itself in the front line during the war years and many men were stationed in the vicinity to prevent surprise German landings from taking place. The worst dangers, however, came from the air, and there were many reported sightings of enemy airships over Aldeburgh and Saxmundham. On the night of 23rd-24th August 1916, for example,

The Marine Parade and beach as depicted on this picture postcard postmarked 1925.

Zeppelin L16 passed over the town and then followed the railway inland, the signal lamps and shining rails being used as an ideal navigational feature by the airship's commander. Later, on 16th June 1917, the Zeppelin L48 was shot down over Theberton, and the remains were brought to Leiston goods yard for disposal as scrap.

THE LNER ERA

In Victorian days successive governments had been opposed to large-scale railway amalgamation schemes on the grounds that competition would (in theory) lead to greater efficiency, but in the changed conditions pertaining after World War One the government itself imposed a comprehensive 'grouping' scheme, this measure being seen as an alternative to outright nationalisation. Thus, on 1st January 1923 the Great Eastern Railway was merged with the Great Central, Great Northern, North Eastern and other companies to form the London & North Eastern Railway.

In LNER days the branch passenger services were typically worked by former Great Eastern Railway 'F3' 2-4-2Ts, while Worsdell 'J15' 0-6-0s handled most of the freight workings. The regular branch engines included 'F3' 2-4-2Ts Nos.8043, 8065, 8071, 8073, 8075 and 8077.

A former Great Central Railway Parker 'F1' 2-4-2T No.5727, was tried out on the Aldeburgh line in 1938 but its sojourn in rural Suffolk was short-lived.

The branch passenger service consisted of seven or eight workings in each direction, with additional services on summer Fridays and Saturdays. In the early 1930s, for example, there were around eight trains each way on weekdays, with extra workings at the weekends; the Sunday service provided just one train in each direction.

This basic pattern of operation persisted throughout the 1930s, and examination of the May 1939 LNER timetable reveals that there were, at that time, 7 up and 7 down trains, rising to 8 up and 8 down on Saturdays. Operations began with the departure of the first up train from Aldeburgh at 7.14 am, the engine which worked this service having been shedded overnight in the branch sub-shed. There were, thereafter, further departures at 8.52 am, 10.42 am, 1.50 pm, 4.12 pm, 5.14 pm and 7.04 pm. In the down direction, balancing services left Saxmundham at 8.09 am, 9.49 am, 11.26 am, 2.35 pm, 4.44 pm, 5.57 pm and 7.37 pm. Through coaches for London were conveyed by three trains each way.

Through coaches were provided to and from Liverpool Street until September

1939, but perhaps the most exotic feature of Aldeburgh branch operation during the 1930s was the provision of regular summer weekday Pullman services from London, the train concerned in this venture being the celebrated 'Eastern Belle'.

First introduced in July 1929, the 'Eastern Belle' utilised Pullman stock that the LNER had inherited in 1923, and for which there would otherwise have been no obvious use. The train was not a scheduled service but a summer special that ran to a varied programme of seaside destinations, and when first introduced the programme was as follows: Mondays – Felixstowe; Tuesdays – Clacton; Wednesdays – Walton-on-Naze; Thursdays – Harwich; Friday – Aldeburgh. The service was expanded the following year to include no less than 18 different resorts.

Alf Marjoram remembers seeing the train on a Saturday when he was playing football near the station. 'The coaches stayed in Aldeburgh station all afternoon while the engine went away. The coaches were put in the goods yard.' This is the only eye-witness account of the working obtained by the authors.

Ordinary train services on the Aldeburgh branch, during the 1920s and 1930s were still being worked by obsolescent short-wheelbase passenger stock. The LNER retained six-wheeled coaches for many years, and in June 1936 a survey published in *The Railway Magazine* revealed that the company was still operating 2,596 short-wheelbase passenger vehicles out of a total fleet of 11,066 coaches, This data (gathered in 1934) revealed that nearly a quarter of all LNER coaches were of short-wheelbase type at a time in which other companies had almost completed the changeover to bogie stock.

Many of the LNER six-wheeled coaches were employed on East Anglian branches such as the Aldeburgh route, a typical formation during the 1920s being four six-wheelers. Bogie vehicles were subsequently drafted into the area in increasing numbers, but it was many years before the older stock was completely eliminated, and there was an inevitable transition period during the early 1930s when trains composed of both bogie and six-wheeled stock could be seen on the Aldeburgh line.

The standard branch formation immediately prior to World War Two consisted of three bogie vehicles, which were usually one brake third, one corridor composite and one ordinary third with the addition, when appropriate, of one or two through carriages to or from Liverpool Street.

THE SECOND WORLD WAR

The early months of World War Two were so quiet that people spoke dismissively of a 'Phoney War'. A nightly blackout was imposed, but otherwise there were few signs of conflict other than the sight of additional numbers of men in uniform. The fall of France in May 1940 revealed Britain's embarrassingly weak position, and in expectation of imminent invasion, a broad swathe of coastal land extending from Sussex to the Wash was declared a restricted area; on 31st May the Government ordered that all signposts and station nameboards should be removed in the hope that this simple ploy might confuse the invaders.

Thelma Block (later Wright) recalls life in the area during the war. She was born in Aldeburgh and lived with her parents in Crabbe Street. The impact of the War was soon felt by the Block Family because they were bombed out and had to move to the High Street. Whilst conditions were perhaps not as bad as many towns and cities, the situation at Aldeburgh was different in that the area was vulnerable to invasion due to its position on the east coast. Consequently 'there seemed to be troops every-

where who had taken over all the empty houses'. They easily outnumbered the local people (of about 400). Many of the large houses, particularly along the Terrace and the Saxmundham Road, together with several hotels were taken over. By the end of 1939, 2/4th Battalion The Essex Regiment had set up a Battalion Headquarters at Aldeburgh Lodge School as part of a strategy to defend the coast. In the following spring, the 9th Battalion The King's Regiment established their HQ at Belstead School. Apart from infiltrating the town, the military set mines on the beach so that certain parts were restricted and "even if you wanted to go on other parts which in reality only amounted to the lifeboat station and the fishing boat slipways, you had to show your identification card".

Thelma remembers that when it was thought an invasion was imminent during 1940, contingency plans were made to evacuate the whole town, and had these been put into effect she would have gone to her Aunt's in Bishops Stortford. Plans were, however, carried out to move all the schoolchildren, and some parents, to Worksop, and special trains are remembered. Ironically, at the outbreak of war, children had been evacuated to the area from London, some arriving by train and some by boat from Dagenham Dock, assembling at the Jubilee Hall near the Lifeboat Station. As we shall see, it is perhaps just as well they returned in the spring of 1940 after the period dubbed 'The Phoney War'.

Thelma worked at the station during part of the war. She remembers security was so tight that people were checked for identification even as they left trains. Ticket issues on the authority of miltary warrants naturally rose as service personnel granted weekend leave took to the trains. Several members of the station staff joined the Local Defence Volunteers (renamed the Home Guard in August 1940). It became officially known in Aldeburgh as 15 Platoon, 8th Battalion Suffolk Home Guard. Aldeburgh's Station Master Bass is believed to have been a sergeant and several of the Aldeburgh staff joined, including Jimmy Gilbert, Billy Botterill, Edgar Bird and the two signalmen Jim Knights and Frank Partridge. During the First World War Jim was a gunner in the Royal Field Artillery and joined the LDV in June 1940. By 1942 he was serving as a Home Guard coast gunner alongside his eldest sons Jimmy and Jake, both of whom went on to

full-time military service. Thelma remembers seeing Mr Bass very optimistically attempting to shoot at an enemy plane with his rifle from the signal box steps! Later the Home Guard manned six-inch naval guns on the beach which had apparently initially been handed over to the Army. Brian Ginger remembers Lengthman 'Choker' Hart patrolling the line at night with his father, both only being armed with sticks. One night when they approached Aldeburgh and were challenged by soldiers, 'Choker' shouted "Don't worry, it's only us!"

The area was attacked on several occasions. Towards the end of 1940, it suffered several 'Hit and Run' raids. The first, on 4th October, caused damage to the Catholic Church and 165 other properties. The following month a similar raid destroyed the Methodist Church, followed by another in which two houses in Thorpeness were destroyed, along with the tennis pavilion in Aldeburgh. One attack in the vicinity of the station was while an Inter-Platoon football match was attacked on the playing fields. Later, a stick of bombs was dropped to the east of the railway line. Fortunately, so far there had been no serious casualties, only treatment for shock. As far as the railway was concerned, the most serious raid was in April 1941 when a bomb hit the gatehouse at Sheepwash Level Crossing between Aldeburgh and Thorpeness. The bomb damaged 100 yards of railway track but fortunately no train was involved. On another occasion Aldeburgh station was struck by machine-gun fire and the walls of the train shed were sprayed with bullets, an incident which may have caused the glass in the roof to become unsafe as it later had to be removed. Windows were also blown out when several mines apparently accidently exploded on the beach. An explosion during April 1941, in Oakley Square where mines were stored, killed four naval ratings working there. The worst air raid was on 15th December 1942 when four bombs were dropped, resulting in the destruction of the Post Office in the High Street and two adjoining houses. In addition, part of the Cottage War Emergency Hospital and buildings in the High Street were damaged. Eleven people lost their lives and 29 were injured. John Hurlock recalls "The only time Saxmundham was hit was when daylight bombers dropped four 250 kgs right in the High Street; all failed to explode. I imagine the crew had failed to 'arm' them. My father was alarmed to see

An Aldeburgh-bound train pulling into Thorpeness Halt behind J15 No. 5459 in September 1947. The porter on the platform appears to be Bill Noy.
R. F. ROBERTS

them in a parked Bedford three-tonner by the sawmills, after (no doubt) de-fusing."

Much of the anti-tank fencing had been constructed by the 9th Cameronians, and when they began leaving the area in November 1941, their Bren gun carriers went by rail and the men travelled by road over the next two days. A Battle School was opened at Belstead School in April 1942 and those training often travelled to Aldeburgh by train.

The railway also played its part with the use of an Armoured Train (often referred to as 'Tin Train'), which began patrolling the railway line between Ipswich and Great Yarmouth in the summer of 1940. The train also patrolled the Aldeburgh Branch and is remembered being stabled during the day at the former Rows Siding at Saxmundham. The train was manned by Polish soldiers who were billeted at nearby Fairfield Road School. Both Brian Ginger and Pamela Strowger (later Smith) remember seeing the train on the line during daylight hours when it was apparently shunted to the goods yard at Aldeburgh before returning.

Towards the end of the war, when the flying bombs were being used and approaching the coast, Jimmy Gilbert recalled working a troop train in the early hours of the morning to Aldeburgh, presumably in connection with coastal defences. During the war he also remembered frequent stops being necessary along the branch to sweep glass out of the coaches, where the windows had been blown out, and often the loco head lamps would also be shattered by the blast of the anti-aircraft guns being used to shoot down the 'doodlebugs'.

Wartime train services continued to operate throughout the 1939-45 emergency period, though on a reduced basis. In 1943, for example, the basic passenger service provided five workings in each direction, with departures from Aldeburgh at 7.15 am, 8.35 am, 12.48 pm, 5.25 pm and 6.39 pm, and return workings from Saxmundham at 8.00 am, 11.03 am, 4.05 pm, 6.10 pm and 8.07 pm. There was no Sunday service, regular Sunday trains having been withdrawn from 3rd November 1940.

EARLY POSTWAR YEARS

The end of the war in Europe was followed by the election of a Labour government which, in accordance with an earlier pledge, nationalised the railway system on 1st January 1948. The Aldeburgh branch thereby became part of British Railways Eastern Region, though, as in 1923, there were no sudden changes and the line from Saxmundham continued to operate much as it had done in pre-war years.

The basic winter weekday train service consisted of half a dozen workings in each direction, rising to seven trains each way in the summer and additional services on Saturdays. Sunday services operated during the summer, with four trains in each direction.

In motive power terms, the branch was still very much a Great Eastern route, the usual engines during early ER days being ex-GER 'F6' 2-4-2Ts and 'J15' 0-6-0s, the latter locomotives being employed on both passenger and freight duties. The regular engines included 'F6' 2-4-2Ts Nos.67220 and 67230, together with 'J15' 0-6-0s Nos.

65447 and 65459. Other 'J15' class 0-6-0s used on the branch during the 1950s included Nos.65440 and 65467, while 'F3' class 2-4-2T No.67127 was also noted on the line at this time.

On a less regular basis, 'E4' class 2-4-0s and 'J20' class 0-6-0s were employed on the Aldeburgh branch on odd occasions, presumably to cover the failure of one of the regular engines; in this context 'J20'

No.64686 worked on the line in August 1951. Another unusual visitor was 'L1' class 2-6-4T No.67705, which worked as far as Leiston on 2nd December 1953 with an engineer's inspection saloon.

A few years earlier, ex-LMS Ivatt '2MT' class 2-6-2T No.41200 was tried out on the line while on loan to Ipswich shed. The engine, which was still lettered 'LMS' on its sides, was first used on Aldeburgh ser-

vices on 4th July 1949, and it worked throughout the remainder of the summer, reappearing in the following year.

The usual formation during the early 1950s was two or three bogie coaches, two vehicles being the norm during the winter months whereas an additional non-corridor vehicle would be added to the branch set during the busier summer period.

The approach to Aldeburgh station viewed from the platform, with the signal box in the centre of the photograph on 13th September 1946.   R. F. ROBERTS

J15 0—6—0 No. 5459 in September 1947 waiting to depart from Aldeburgh. The driver and fireman are thought to have been Jack Runnacles and Maurice Holman.
R. F. ROBERTS

THE ROUTE DESCRIBED

Saxmundham, the junction for Aldeburgh, was a relatively large rural station on the East Suffolk line, some 91 miles from Liverpool Street and $22\frac{1}{2}$ miles from Ipswich. Opened, along with the rest of the ESR line on 1st June 1859, it was provided with siding accommodation for handling coal and local agricultural traffic, together with up and down platforms and substantial brick station buildings. Like other East Suffolk stations, its two platforms were widely staggered, the down (northbound)

Saxmundham station photographed from the down platform in September 1947 clearly showing the staggered arrangement of the platforms. R. F. ROBERTS

The 7.50 a.m. branch train ready to depart from the down platform at Saxmundham on 2nd June 1952. The engine, 2–4–2T No. 67220, was a member of the F6 class introduced in 1911.
J. J. SMITH

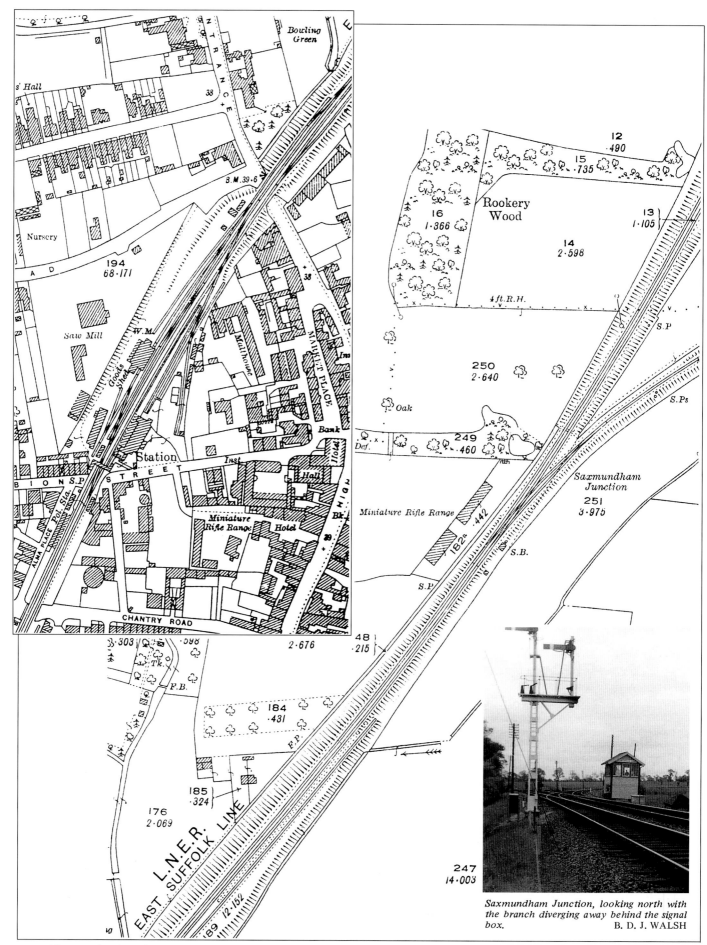

Saxmundham Junction, looking north with the branch diverging away behind the signal box. B. D. J. WALSH

platform being situated to the south of its counterpart on the up side of the line, the two separated by an intervening level crossing which carried Albion Street across the running lines, and the main station buildings were sited on the up platform, nearest the town centre. A short bay was provided on the up side, but branch trains normally ran to or from the main platforms.

Leaving Saxmundham, branch trains followed the East Suffolk 'main line' northwards for a short distance before turning eastwards onto their own line at Saxmundham Junction, which was controlled from a standard Great Eastern 'Type Two' gabled signal box with 17 levers. After diverging, the branch immediately singled, and, climbing at 1 in 58, trains set off across open Suffolk countryside towards Aldeburgh and the sea.

Heading due east, the route traversed picturesque, though unspectacular terrain with few visual features to dispel an initial hint of monotony. After a mile, trains crossed a road on the level, and the railway then turned rightwards onto a more southeasterly heading. A lonely country lane ran

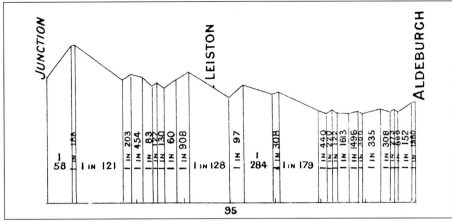

Approaching Knodishall level crossing from Leiston.
B. D. J. WALSH

Approaching Westhouse level crossing from Leiston.

B. D. J. WALSH

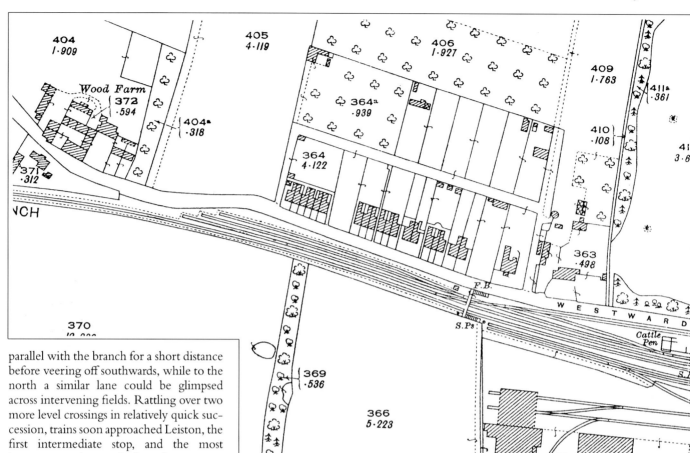

parallel with the branch for a short distance before veering off southwards, while to the north a similar lane could be glimpsed across intervening fields. Rattling over two more level crossings in relatively quick succession, trains soon approached Leiston, the first intermediate stop, and the most important station on the branch.

Situated a little under 4 miles (3 miles 74 chains) from Saxmundham and $4\frac{1}{4}$ miles from Aldeburgh, Leiston was roughly half way along the branch. It was equipped with a single platform and a crossing loop which enabled two goods trains or one goods and one passenger train to pass.

The passenger platform was sited on the down, or north, side of the line, with goods sidings to the west and Garrett's extensive engineering works to the south. Leiston's track layout was more complex, than might have been expected, accentuated by the connections to Garrett's factory and its extensive internal railway system.

In earlier days, Garrett's had relied upon horses, gravity and a cable-worked incline for their internal shunting operations, but after an accident involving a pair of loose wagons in 1929, the firm purchased a four-wheeled Aveling Porter geared shunting locomotive called *Sirapite* (Works No. 6158), and this curious machine could often be seen at work in the factory sidings. Looking rather like a traction engine on rails (which indeed it was), *Sirapite* was built in 1906, and it had just one cylinder mounted horizontally on top of the boiler; it was ideally suited for light shunting duties within the works – though it is perhaps

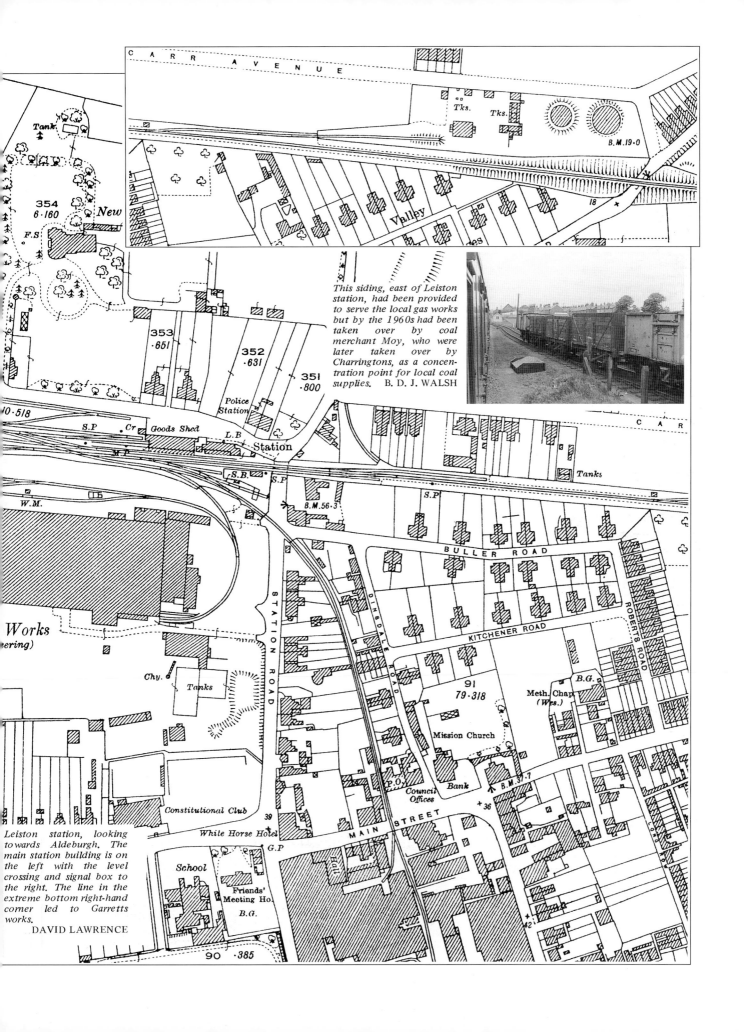

C A R R A V E N U E

Tank.

354
6·160

New

F.S.

Tks.

Tks.

B.M.19·0

Valley

18

353
·651

352
·631

351
·800

Police
Station

This siding, east of Leiston station, had been provided to serve the local gas works but by the 1960s had been taken over by coal merchant Moy, who were later taken over by Charringtons, as a concentration point for local coal supplies. B. D. J. WALSH

10·518

S.P.   Cr   Goods Shed   L.B   Station

M.P.

S.B.   S.P.

B.M.56·3

Tanks

S.P.

C A R

W.M.

BULLER ROAD

Works
ering)

Chy.   Tanks

KITCHENER ROAD

91
79·318

Meth. Chap.
(Wes.)

B.G.

ROBERTS ROAD

STATION ROAD

DINGDALE ROAD

Mission Church

Constitutional Club

39

White Horse Hotel

G.P.

P.O.

Council
Offices

Bank

B.M.37·7

+ 36

B.M.

Leiston station, looking towards Aldeburgh. The main station building is on the left with the level crossing and signal box to the right. The line in the extreme bottom right-hand corner led to Garretts works.

DAVID LAWRENCE

School

Friends'
Meeting Ho

B.G.

MAIN STREET

Hall

+42

90   ·385

surprising that Garrett's should have purchased an engine from a rival engineering company!

Heading eastwards away from Leiston, the line passed over a level crossing and rapidly approached the North Sea, but before reaching the coast, trains rumbled across the only underbridge on the branch; this modest structure carried a minor road beneath the line.

Running through a short section of cutting, the railway then turned through ninety degrees and crossed two minor roads on the level before straightening-out onto a southerly heading for the final two miles to Aldeburgh and passing an isolated goods siding at Sizewell crossing.

Entering a tract of attractive, open marshland, down trains ran over another level crossing, after which they came to rest beside the single platform at Thorpeness Halt, $6\frac{1}{4}$ miles from Saxmundham. Here passenger and staff accommodation was provided by grounded bodies of ancient Great Eastern carriages whilst a single siding trailing from the down direction on

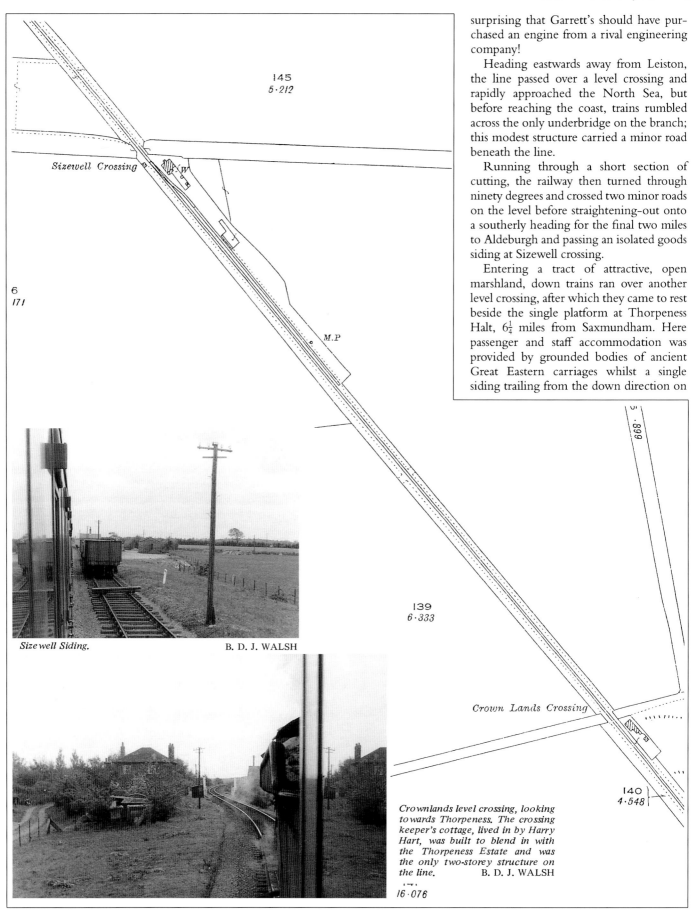

Sizewell Crossing

145
5·212

6
171

M.P

139
6·333

Crown Lands Crossing

140
4·548

Sizewell Siding.   B. D. J. WALSH

Crownlands level crossing, looking towards Thorpeness. The crossing keeper's cottage, lived in by Harry Hart, was built to blend in with the Thorpeness Estate and was the only two-storey structure on the line.   B. D. J. WALSH

16·076

the west side of the line was provided for goods traffic.

Thorpeness itself occupied a coastal site, a little under one mile from the railway. As mentioned earlier, this seaside settlement was a purpose-built holiday resort which dated, in the main, from the 1930s. Although not perhaps to everyone's taste, the resort contained a wealth of 1930s-style buildings, one of the most striking being the 'Country Club', which featured a massive gothic-style water tower. Nearby, a towering folly known (appropriately enough) as 'The House in the Cloud', provided superb views across the surrounding countryside, whilst the Church of St Mary dated from as recently as 1938.

Leaving Thorpeness Halt, down trains ran due south towards their destination,

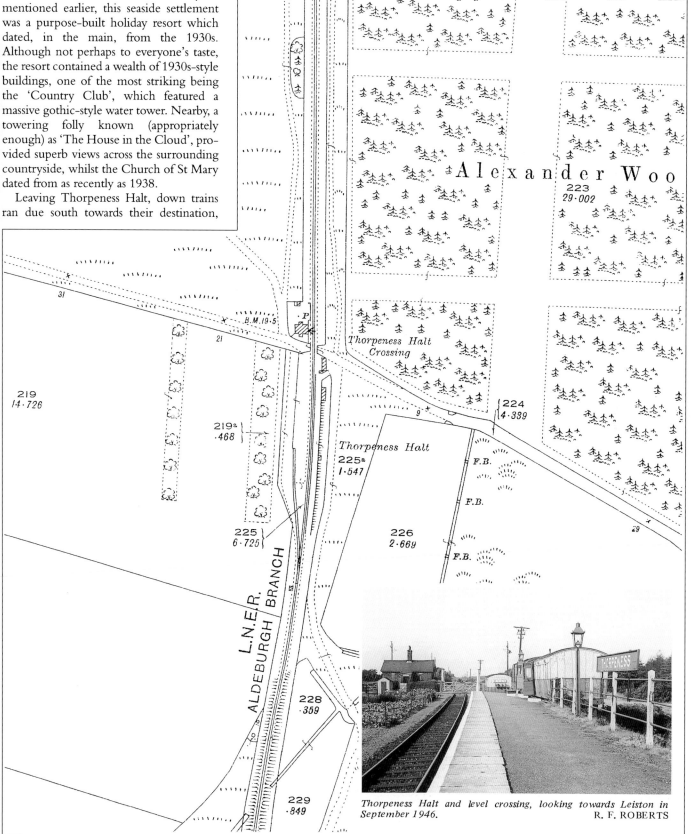

Thorpeness Halt and level crossing, looking towards Leiston in September 1946.
R. F. ROBERTS

and, with a stretch of open water known as The Meare visible to the left, the 20 minute journey from Saxmundham drew to a close. Slowing for the final approach to Aldeburgh, trains rattled over the facing points at the northern end of the station, and with sidings now visible on both sides of the running line, the eight and a quarter mile rural journey came to an end. The simple terminus was provided with a brick-built station building and train shed, goods shed, engine shed, water tower and signal box.

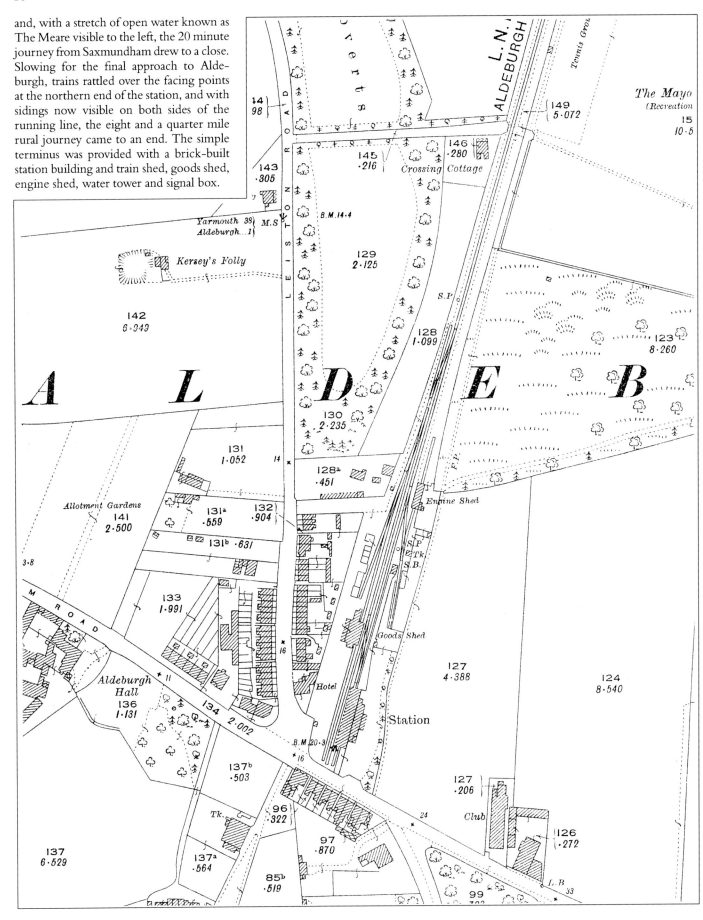

ALDEBURGH

Aldeburgh station and approach road in the early 1950s. The W. H. Smith & Son station bookstall had been situated on the platform just inside the train shed more or less on the opposite side of the wall to its final position. The bookstall covered a double door in the wall which had earlier been used for access to the platform. However, by the time of this picture, there was an alternative way alongside. It was here that fish traffic was taken on to the platform for loading. There was only one door into the bookstall at the front. Inside on the left was a counter with cigarettes and sweets behind. There was an office at the back accessible via a door on the left. Newspapers and magazines were sold on the right, with stationery items against the right-hand window. Ray Mills was Smith's local manager and in charge of Aldeburgh and Saxmundham. Certainly by the early postwar years, supplies of newspapers, etc, for Aldeburgh station were collected by Ray from the newspaper train at Saxmundham and taken by road, calling at Griffiths of Leiston and Millers of Aldeburgh (both on an agency basis). Ray had started in the bookstall at Saxmundham during the 1930s, working for George Godfrey, the then manager. After wartime service, he took charge at Aldeburgh, and when Mr. Godfrey was promoted to Manager at King's Lynn, Ray was based at Saxmundham and in overall charge at Aldeburgh, Saxmundham and Halesworth. By the early 1950s, Sylvia Smith was in charge at Aldeburgh where she was assisted by Diana Sones and up to five boys and girls on delivery rounds. She worked from 6.0 a.m. to 7.30 a.m. sorting the papers ready for delivery, and after breakfast returned from 8.0 until 5.30, with an hour for lunch. She usually got a half day on Saturdays.

Porter Billy Botterill at the roadside entrance. He appears to have spent most of his working life at the station and is remembered for his wonderful sense of humour.

CTY. TOM STEBBINGS

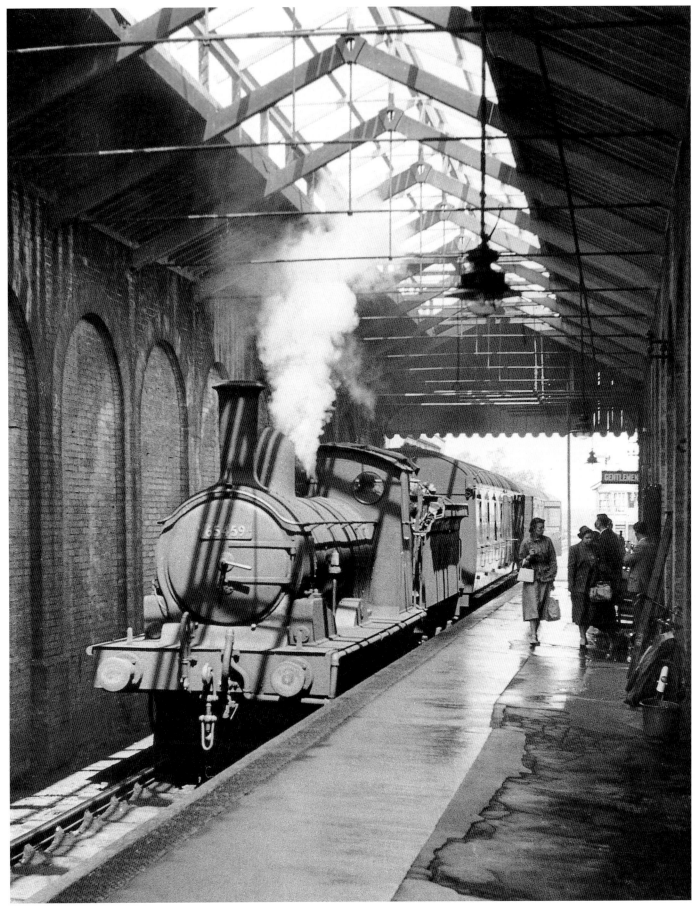

J15 class No. 65459 shortly after arrival with the 12.30 p.m. from Saxmundham on 26th July 1953.

R. E. VINCENT

STAFF AT ALDEBURGH

Amongst staff remembered were:

Station Masters – Mr L.W. Bass, E.R. Wright, B.L. Reeve, and J. Carter. Dennis Eastaugh and later Peter Girling when the line was administered from Leiston.

Clerical Staff – Sid Beales, Thelma Block (later Wright), Marie Block (Thelmas sister), Pamela Strowger (later Smith), who remembers following Thelma in May 1956, Ivan Watling and Basil Barlow who is thought to have been the last clerk.

Porters – Billy Botterill, Pat Barley, Tom Church-yard, Theodore 'Skinny' White, George Ward, Ossie Everitt.

Motor Driver – Edgar Bird.

Signalmen – Jim Knights, Frank Partridge, Henry Vale, Michael Beamish and Hubert Havers. Tony Spatchett and Monty Baskett regularly covered on relief.

Guards – Bill Wright, Walter Barnes and later Bill Noy. When the diesel multiple units arrived, the workings were covered from Ipswich.

Aldeburgh's main station building was a two-storey, hip-roofed structure, resembling those at Leiston, Saxmundham, and other former East Suffolk stations. Like Leiston, it was simple to the point of austerity, but its classical proportions added an element of sophistication. Entering the building from the east, travellers passed through a central doorway, with two flanking windows on either side and five symmetrically-placed windows on the first floor, matching 'pavilions' extended from each end of the building, and the hipped roof was pierced by two chimney stacks of equal height. The centrally-placed doorway was protected by a small canopy, but on the opposite side of the building the entire facade was covered by an overall roof which protected the the platform and the main platform road. The roof was supported on substantial retaining walls, and a clerestory was provided to facilitate smoke emission. The left-hand door in the main station building led to Edgar Bird's hallway, kitchen and stairs to his home above the station. These rooms had originally been the Station Master's home but quite when they ceased being used for this purpose is unclear. However, it is known that Mr. Orford, who was Station Master between the wars, lived with his family in Fawcett Road. The central double doors led into the booking hall with the office to the left and waiting rooms/ladies toilets to the right. The ticket window was in the centre of the dividing wall with a stable-type door on the right (platform side). Immediately facing on entering the office were telephones and at one time the telegraphic instruments. On the left were the scales for weighing parcels. There was no parcels office as such, the booking clerk sorted the consignments between the booking office and hall, using the scales to check the weights of outward packages for charging purposes. The ticket rack was to the right of the ticket window (i.e. the station approach road side) and finally, against the road side window, was a desk and chair. Alongside the desk was a sealed door which had at one time led to the adjoining hallway, but certainly by the Second World War is only remembered as having a coat hook on the back for the gas masks. On the other side of the booking hall, a door directly opposite the door to the booking office led to the general waiting room and then into the ladies room and toilet. Both waiting rooms had large centrally situated tables and an assortment of chairs. The gents, Station Master's office and lamp room were accessible from the platform. Comparison with an Edwardian view reveals minor changes which took place over the years. Certainly the corner supports to the train shed at the buffer stops end had lost their ornate tops, possibly following wartime damage when the glass in the top of the train shed was also removed. The canopy at the road side entrance lost its valancing during the Second World War when an army lorry accidentally struck it. Off the picture to the right were the station gardens, tended largely by porter Billy Botterill. The BR(ER) Staff Magazine records that '. . . under Bill's care Aldeburgh has never failed to gain less than a first class prize. The station received its first special award in 1923 and had an unbroken sequence of specials from 1929 up to the outbreak of war . . . '

The station from the air in June 1920, with the Saxmundham Road running from the bottom right to top left and the Station Hotel set back on the edge of the goods yard. The edge of the main part of the town is at the top of the photograph.
SIMMONS AEROFILMS

Looking north from the buffer stops with the bookstall on the right and the platform entrance gate. Fire buckets are visible just inside the train shed. A tap provided nearby was used by the booking clerk to fill up a kettle for the porters' room, visible along the platform in the distance. Next was a door to the Station Master's office, then the lamp room, the platform side door to the booking hall and, at the far end, the gents toilet. The signal box is visible in the distance and the goods yard and goods shed to the left. The white paint marks on the corner of the train shed were a legacy from wartime blackout.

This picture, taken just inside the entrance to the goods yard, features the train shed wall and the goods shed and office. The office was accessible from a set of steps on the left (obscured by a trailer) and was provided with a desk and chair which faced the window. A door led from the office direct to the shed deck whilst a store underneath the office, accessible via a trap door, was used to hold valuable items overnight. Incidentally, there were no cattle pens although it is believed animals had been loaded and unloaded at the dock near the engine shed in earlier years. It appears a coal office had existed near the siding alongside the shed road, but during the 1950s, coal merchant Moy had built a brick office at the yard entrance. The tractor was almost certainly delivering sugar beet for despatch. DEREK CLAYTON

GOODS TRAFFIC

GENERAL 'SMALLS'

Apart from regular 'smalls' items delivered by Edgar Bird, Timothy, White & Taylor received a van load of containers from their Leeds warehouse once a month. The local pubs received beer in barrels from Stewart and Paterson of Norwich, which arrived on the branch goods. The International Stores also received supplies from their warehouses. Cigarettes arrived in sealed vans from Wills of Bristol.

FISH

Whilst herring, plaice and lobster were caught locally, most of the railborne supplies consisted of sprats despatched during the late Autumn until January/February and dealt with by Lawrence Baggott, a local dealer who is remembered as a 'great character'. Live eels were also despatched to Billingsgate. Although, as already stated, a van was sometimes attached to the branch train, traffic was more regularly loaded onto the brake vans. When there was no Sunday train service, Thelma remembers coming on duty to assist Edgar Bird 'sheet' the traffic, which he roaded to Saxmundham for loading to a main-line train. Empty boxes were returned to Aldeburgh either as goods traffic or in the passenger brakes.

FARM PRODUCE/SUGAR BEET

Farmers used the railway and apart from the despatch of sugar beet and corn, also received supplies of animal food stuffs. Scotch potato seeds arrived with corn seed in the same truck as a composite load (at a reduced charge). Incidentally, the railway operated a sack hire arrangement for local farmers. Most sugar beet was grown at Aldeburgh Hall, Grange and Church Farms and dealt with in the same way as at Saxmundham.

COAL

Moy

Thomas Moy Ltd had a branch at Aldeburgh with an office in the goods yard during the 1950s having previously traded at 112 High Street and at the station between about 1900 and 1920. Peter Knights worked for Moy when they were at Aldeburgh in the postwar years, when they subsequently took over from Cundy and Saint. Most of the coal came from Derbyshire. Supplies were domestic with some bulk work for schools. Apart

Charles Douglas Joy's home at 'The Priory', 234 High Street, Aldeburgh.
CTY. DOROTHY CADY

from Aldeburgh, deliveries were made as far as Thorpeness. The company (part of the Rickett Cockerell group) was later amalgamated with Charrington and, as already stated, dealt with supplies at Leiston.

Peter Knights worked for coal merchant Moy at Aldeburgh from the mid-1950s, collecting supplies from Aldeburgh station and delivering locally. Hubert Smith was in charge of a company office at Leiston where coal orders were received by

Looking towards the buffer stops with what appears to be a parcels van which may have been left there for fish traffic. The building on the left was the porters' room, which contained a table and benches on each side. There were lockers at the back and a stove. In earlier years, the room is said to have been used to heat foot warmers for the branch carriages. By the time of this picture it was also used to store cleaning equipment. The gents toilet door, seen above the fence line, was reached via an archway from the platform. When running round, the coaches had first to be set back clear of the engine release crossover in the foreground. The Railway Hotel, just visible outside the station, was known locally as 'The Ram' and nearby Leiston Road (where several members of the branch staff and their families lived) as 'Ram Row', both names evidently legacies from the days when local farmers used to herd their sheep in the area.

The goods shed was, like the station building, substantially built of brick. The cart entrance was covered by a projecting canopy, and the internal loading platform was equipped with a 1 ton 10 cwt hand crane; the building had a gabled roof, with raised parapets at each end and decorative features known as 'kneelers' on each corner (i.e. to form a neat termination at the lower end of each parapet). By this time, most of the goods traffic was being dealt with at the end of the shed road, including some of the coal traffic. The annexe to the goods shed may have been a weighbridge at one time but certainly by the 1940s was used by Edgar Bird's wife as a wash room, and a 'copper' was fitted inside. Any wagons requiring the use of a weighbridge had to be sent to Leiston to be dealt with.

Peter Strowger, who took them to Aldeburgh as appropriate.

Peter and Frank Lomax worked in the goods yard bagging coal direct from railway wagons onto 3-ton Ford lorries for delivery or for storage at the wharves. They checked the weight with portable scales. The lorries were painted light green with yellow lettering.

Up to two or three wagons arrived each day. "We dealt mainly with Gedley and Glidsworth Collieries." Anthracite was received from South Wales and coke was collected from Ipswich gas works.

Joy/Saint

Charles Douglas Joy had taken over the coal business of C. H. Chandler at The Priory, 234 High Street, Aldeburgh by about 1915. He was born at West Molesey, Surrey in 1884 and when he left school worked for a local market gardener. He married Louisa Chapman, a local girl, in 1915, following which they went to Aldeburgh and took over Chandler's business. The sequence of events is not now clear, but it appears that his father Charles, who had set up his own market garden at Ivydene, Park Road, Aldeburgh, assisted his son financially with his new venture. It may even have been in part a marriage gift.

Charles Douglas continued to trade as H.W. Joy, Coal, Coke and Firewood (late C. H.

Chandler) at Ivydene from around 1910 and by the 1920s at 234 High Street, which was also his home, where they had twin daughters, Dorothy and Gladys. Sadly, their father did not enjoy good health and died in August 1926 aged only 42 years. He had been a popular figure in Aldeburgh. He was prominent in the local council, was a coastguard and served on the lifeboat as well as being a member of the St. John Ambulance and in charge of the ambulance. He served in the local Special Constabulary during the Great War and was a Worshipful Master in the local Freemasons.

Following her husband's death, Louisa carried on the business with assistance from Percy Fish, who had covered the delivery work, having also worked for Chandlers for a short while. Even her daughters helped out. Dorothy recalls during the Depression years, dealing with small amounts of coal for the poor. "People literally pleaded with my mother to let them have coal." Louisa found it difficult to run the business.

Joan Fish remembers her father Percy driving a horse and cart for Joy and later Saint, delivering domestic coal as far as the Saxmundham Road. She had fond memories of her father's horse, Dobbin, which was kept at stables in King Street and hauled a light and heavy van, being grazed near Marsh Cottage (between the High Street and the sea front). The horse and vans were later replaced with a motor lorry.

In the late 1920s, Louisa's nephew, Claude Saint, who had moved from Leicester to Aldeburgh for health reasons, helped out. Claude married Vera Kemp, a local girl, in 1937 and lived at Victoria Road and, by the Second World War, Lee Road, where he ran the business from the front room after the sale of the High Street premises in the late 1930s. The business was absorbed by Moy in the 1950s.

Cundy

Ernest Cundy's business was established at 111 High Street in the 1920s and remained trading until the Second World War, using only motor transport. It appears part of Cundy's business may have passed to a Mr Wright (through marriage) who traded in coal in a small way at the Leiston Road.

Ward

Bert Ward was also established at the same period as Cundy and traded from the High Street and station. By the late 1930s, local directories indicate his address as only at the railway station.

Knights

Knights traded from the Leiston Road but little has been established about him.

Behind the goods yard, the north end of the site was used by local builders Wm. C. Reade, with access via the Leiston Road. There was no vehicular access to the station here. The points near the signal box led to the loco shed siding via a dock which ran behind the fence line on the right. The water tower is also visible on the right.

TRANSPORT TREASURY

The signal box was a typical GER gable-roof design, incorporating semi-prefabricated timber components, with the door and external stairway situated at the south end of the cabin. The building housed a 21-lever Stevens frame and was clad in horizontal weather boarding, with a tall, stovepipe chimney extending through the slated roof. The name 'ALDEBURGH' was displayed above the windows at each end of the box. The signalling arrangements at Aldeburgh were surprisingly simple, and apart from the usual home, starting and distant signals, there were a number of ground discs controlling the run-round loop and the engine siding.   DEREK CLAYTON & COLLECTION R. K. BLENCOWE

DAILY ROUTINES

After a short spell at Leiston, Thelma Block (later Wright) transferred to Aldeburgh as a passenger clerk, where she replaced Sid Beales (when he transferred to Leiston) and she remained there until 1953 when she left the railway to get married. She remembers coming on duty at 6.55 am and booking the first train, then worked until 1.15 pm, overlapping with the late turn who worked from 1.0 to 7 15. Sunday duty was covered on overtime as a split shift from 9.30 am to midday and from 6.0 pm to 8.0. The Station Master stepped in if the clerks were not available. There were not many regular travellers, "only a few for Garretts at Leiston". There were no grammar and secondary schools in Aldeburgh at this time, so children travelled on the 8.40 am to Leiston, returning on the 4.15 pm from Saxmundham. However, around 1953/4 they travelled by bus (it is said that the children had been tampering with the train). Apart from dealing with passenger bookings and accounts as well as the parcels traffic, the booking clerk paid out the wages each week. The timesheets were certified as correct by the SM and sent to Ipswich for authorisation. Pay day was on Friday and the SM was responsible for collecting the cash from the bank and passing it to the booking clerk who made up the wage packets. During the end of the late shift when Billy Botterill had gone home, the clerk also collected tickets from arriving passengers. The goods work was covered by a goods clerk who also covered as necessary in the booking office. At about 8.30 am, the parcels delivery sheets were prepared in the booking hall (there was no parcels office) and Thelma 'sheeted' the outwards consignments as read out to her by Edgar Bird, the motor driver, who also collected and delivered the goods traffic. When Edgar returned from his rounds, Thelma calculated charges for outwards traffic which were despatched in the brakes of the branch trains. Edgar lived above the station with his wife in what had been the Station Master's home at one time. He appears to have lived there from between the wars and had been a porter and later a horse delivery man at Saxmundham.

Porter Billy Botterill is remembered as a great character who had been at the station at least since the 1920s. Billy and 'Waffy' Fryer (later a motor driver at Saxmundham) had worked together at Aldeburgh in earlier years, both starting straight from school. Apparently they became so mischievous they had to be parted and 'Waffy' was moved away! Billy worked a middle shift and was on duty to deal with the second train of the day. By the 1950s he worked until midday and then went to Thorpeness and relieved Bill Noy there for the afternoon until Bill returned in the early evening. Meanwhile the goods porter covered the platform work at Aldeburgh. Thelma remembers Billy as a "lovely man" but always up to some antic or other. A typical situation was when he used to help

Looking north again, but this time from the dock behind the main platform, with the engine shed, water tower and coal stage on the right. The engine shed line extended through the shed and, in addition to the inspection pit visible, there was another inside the shed. Part of Edgar Bird's garden is seen on the right. Edgar was a keen gardener and apart from vegetables grew flowers in his own garden which complemented those tended by porter Billy Botterill along the side of the station approach.   DEREK CLAYTON

himself to coal from the engine shed supply and wheeled it away to the porters' room using a barrow. When caught by one of the drivers, he was told "he would be reported for taking coal using a barrow", to which he replied "In that case I'll use a trolley next time". On another occasion he tried to persuade Thelma to pull faces at one of the engine drivers – "He might then throw coal at you!" He took great pride in the station gardens which won many prizes. In later years, when Thelma and her family went off on holiday, Billy usually placed detonators on the line to ensure they had a good send off! Billy is still fondly remembered in Aldeburgh – he was so very much a part of the scene.

Pat Barley, a porter during the mid 1950s, remembers working a middle shift from about 8.0 am to 5.0 pm together with Billy Botterill. Pat, Billy and motor driver Edgar Bird took it in turns to cover Sunday duty, and during the middle of the day, when there was no train service, the porter cleaned the coaches in the platform. Pat remembers sweeping out each carriage compartment, then washing down the exterior using a long-handled brush. The windows were evidently brought to a shine using 'Teepol'. The side away from the platform was cleaned with the aid of a pair of steps. During the week, apart from assisting Billy Botterill on the platform, Pat spent part of his shift in the goods yard assisting with the shunting and loading/unloading of wagons. As already stated,

the delivery lorry was driven by Edgar Bird whose rounds extended as far as Thorpeness. If a bulky item was being collected or delivered, Pat travelled with Edgar and assisted. He also covered at Thorpeness Halt and Sheepwash Crossing when staff there were on holiday or sick.

Michael Beamish (the son of Cliff Beamish, the Leiston ganger) was a signalman at Aldeburgh following the introduction of diesel multiple units in 1956 and recalls the daily routine continuing very much in the same way as the 1940s. He cycled in from Knodishall (between Saxmundham and Leiston) and unlocked the booking hall after unlocking the signal box where the station keys were kept. He then returned to open the signal box and awaited the arrival of an empty DMU from Ipswich, which incidentally conveyed newpapers as far as Saxmundham. The first train was dealt with by the signalman and the guard; Billy Botterill came in for a middle turn and apparently also dealt with the goods work as by this time he did not cover Thorpeness because it had been reduced to the status of a halt. Edgar Bird still covered the delivery of goods and parcels. The clerk Basil Barlow covered a middle shift and was apparently responsible for all the clerical work. During the evening the signalman was the only member of staff on duty and closed the station before going home.

Coaling and watering facilities were available beside the engine shed spur, the coal stage being merely a rectangular brick platform topped by a sleeper-built stockade. The water column consisted of a tall cast-iron pillar to which was attached a flexible hose, while the adjacent water tower was a brick-built structure supporting a raised metal tank. There were grounds for thinking that this small brick building may have been added after the Great Eastern takeover in 1862 (similar or substantially similar water towers being found at various other GER stations including Braintree, Thaxted and Wells-next-the-Sea). Water supply was evidently something of a problem at Aldeburgh, and it was necessary for the GER to pump supplies to the tank; in this context it is interesting to discover that Mr. G. Airey started his career in the Locomotive Department as a 'pumper' at Aldeburgh in July 1872. It is believed that the 'pumper' also helped with cleaning and other menial duties. Mr. Airey was transferred to Ipswich as a cleaner in 1874, and had become a driver by 1885 (he later worked on the Walton-on-Naze and Clacton lines). 5th June 1954.
COLLECTION R. K. BLENCOWE

The engine shed was similar to the goods shed, with a gabled roof and raised parapets at each end. It could accommodate either a tank engine or small tender engine. There were doors at both ends, the shed being a 'through' structure which spanned an engine siding. The shed was illuminated by small-paned windows with slightly-arched brick heads, and office and mess room accommodation was provided in a small lean-to extension that adjoined the east wall of the main structure. The lean-to annexe to the engine shed was an office/mess room where the senior driver did his paperwork. It was also used for meal breaks and by some of the relief men from Ipswich to sleep in when covering early turns. A stove was at the far side. The shed was the residence of an owl which slept during the day in the rafters. There were also mice and the night man recalled it was often very eery and "one could only hear the sound of the sea". Station Master Bass had allotments alongside the line beyond the shed, and when he was needed at the station, the signalman operated the starting signal several times to attract his attention! 5th June 1954.
COLLECTION R. K. BLENCOWE

THORPENESS

Bill Noy was the porter in charge and lived with his family in the crossing house nearby. He was born at Sizewell Common in December 1903 and joined the Great Eastern Railway in October 1918. By 1921 he was a porter at Leiston. During the 1920s, however, work became short in the area (presumably due to the Depression) and he worked at Stratford, East London, for a while as a carriage cleaner. He had returned to the area by the early 1930s when he was a horse delivery driver at Ipswich, also apparently dealing with horse shunting, and met his wife, who worked at Marks and Spencer, during his rounds. He was passed out as a lorry driver in December 1935 and covered delivery work at Framlingham and later Saxmundham where, he delivered principally animal foodstuffs around the country area. The Noys were by this time living at Sizewell but from 1944 lived at Kelsale where Mrs Noy looked after North Green Level Crossing, on the main line north of Saxmundham. Bill took over at Thorpeness in 1946, on the retirement of Harry Rice who had worked there since at least the 1920s, and remained until the station was reduced to a halt, when he became a branch guard for a short while and later covered at Saxmundham Road

Looking west to Thorpeness station on the Thorpeness to Aldringham Road, with the crossing keeper's cottage in the distance on the Leiston side of the gates. The station was on the near side of the line.

The entrance to the Halt photographed from the Thorpeness to Aldringham Road. The building on the extreme right, a former 1883 second class coach body, was used as a storage shed for parcels. Next was the booking office (formed from an 1880 third class vehicle) and next to this a waiting room from an 1897 first class carriage. The other waiting room is also visible at the end of the platform on the left.

A closer view of the entrance and parcels shed.

One of these vehicles masqueraded as a waiting room while its companion provided booking and staff facilities; the third vehicle was used as a store. Although precise identification was difficult, all three coaches were former six-wheelers, dating from the 1880's; the booking office and storage shed were either seconds or thirds, but the waiting room was slightly more luxurious, being an ex-first class vehicle with only four (as opposed to five) doors on each side. Internally, it was equipped with typical waiting room seats and a solidly constructed wooden floor; posters adorned its walls, and a dark blue ER enamel sign informed passengers that the venerable vehicle was Thorpeness Halt's Waiting Room. At night, the halt was lit by oil lamps resting in traditional, Great Eastern-type glass lanterns, which could be distinguished from those of other pre-Grouping lines by their noticeably square profile. The platform was fenced with tubular rail fencing, and there were some attractive flower gardens on what had formerly been a patch of waste ground to the west of the platform.

P. J. KELLEY

Inside the booking office at Thorpeness, with Arthur Cant, a motor driver from Leiston, who relieved on a regular basis.

B. D. J. WALSH

level crossing. Following a motor driving refresher in March 1963, he took over delivery work from Edgar Bird of Aldeburgh when he retired, and continued with branch goods delivery work (by then concentrated at Leiston and later Ipswich) until he left railway service in October 1966. Bill was very proud of his work and received several station garden and best kept station certificates also safe driving diplomas and awards. In the early postwar period there were early and late porters but by the 1950s Bill covered all trains until the early afternoon when a porter from Aldeburgh relieved, Bill returning in the evening to deal with the last trains of the day.

GOODS TRAFFIC

The only traffic remembered was sugar beet despatched in the season, mainly to Ipswich. It was dealt with in the same way as the traffic at Saxmundham and the paperwork handled by Aldeburgh who were responsible for the administration of the station.

Bill Noy cleaning one of the oil lamps.

CTY. BARBARA AND MARY NOY

The view towards Leiston shows the crossing cottage which consisted of four rooms with a porch on the road side. Even during the early 1950s, conditions were primitive, water being drawn from a well, and there was only a privvy at the bottom of the garden. The end of the goods siding features on the left and the station garden, opposite the platform, won many prizes over the years.

COLLECTION
R. K. BLENCOWE

Another view nearer to the station buildings. A foot-path ran behind the platform alongside Thorpeness Golf Course. This path and the golf course were dissected by the Thorpeness to Aldringham Road which crossed the railway at the level crossing.

P. J. KELLEY

SIZEWELL SIDING

It is said the siding had been provided for the receipt and despatch of Highland cattle brought to the area for grazing on the local commons. Towards the end of the Second World War, however, train loads of rubble and huts arrived which were used to provide access and accommodation at the numerous anti-aircraft gun sites being provided to counter the flying bomb menace. The rubble formed access roads and the huts were used by personnel at the sites. After the war, the siding's principal role was the receipt of coal for the Leiston Co-operative Society. Ivan Watling recalled Mr Denny used to make periodic visits to check regarding demurrage, also whether space rental arrangements were being adhered to.

SIZEWELL POWER STATION

A late traffic development at Leiston was the arrival of constructional material at Leiston for the building of the power station at Sizewell. Special trains ran and were unloaded in the back road of the goods yard. Additional staff were drafted in from Ipswich to deal with the traffic and crane driver Cyril Pennock and motor driver Tony Chatten are remembered.

When opened on 29th July 1914, Thorpeness had been a passenger-only stopping place, but a single goods siding was added on the west side of the running line in May 1921 for coal or other freight traffic. The siding trailed from the down direction and was only served by down trains to Aldeburgh.   H. C. CASSERLEY

Sizewell siding viewed from a passing train. As mentioned in the text, this was used by the Leiston Cooperative Society for the receipt of coal. Sizewell level crossing is seen in the background.
B. D. J. WALSH

It was reported by the Board of Trade in June 1892 that a new 35-lever signal cabin had been erected. The work was undertaken in conjunction with remodelling work, details of which are unclear.

B. D. J. WALSH

STAFF AT LEISTON

Amongst staff remembered were:

Station Masters – Dennis Eastaugh and in the final years Peter Girling.

Clerical Staff – Chief Goods Clerk Albert Denny, later Sidney Beales, Goods Clerk Cliff Lilley (assisted Albert Denny), Peter Blowers, Junior Goods Clerk Ivan Watling, later Pamela Strowger (later Smith), Booking Clerks Joan Meadows, Rex Debenham, George Woolnough, Horace Parker, John White and Geoff Smith.

Porters – During the war, Daisy Sharland and Annie Taylor. Sid Skippings (a relief man from Ipswich), Owen Allcock, Percy Cooper, Les Ashford and Bob Cross.

Porter/Shunter – 'Punch' Goodwin, later Harry Sawyer who was 'referred to by Pamela Strowger as 'Mr Yardmaster'.

Motor Driver – Arthur Cant and in the final years Bill Noy.

Signalmen – Arthur Goddard, Bill Boreham (later at Saxmundham), Peter Spall (who took over from Bill) and Brian Ginger.

Relief Crossing Keeper – Fred Ginger, who covered the manned level crossings under Leiston's control.

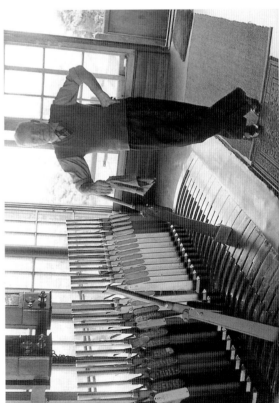

Inside the signal box, with signalman Arthur Goddard, who, along with Harry Sawyer, was one of the longest serving members of staff at Leiston. Arthur was born in 1895 and joined the Great Eastern Railway in 1911 as a lad porter at Saxmundham, putting earlier experience on a farm to good use in dealing with the large amounts of animal traffic. By the time of the Great War, he was a shunter at Ipswich. He had taken a keen interest in signalling and, after war service in 1919, became a signalman at Leiston, where he remained until his retirement in 1961. Even then, he returned to cover during the summer months until the withdrawal of the passenger service in 1966. The box was kept scrupulously clean and the floor was mopped using water heated on the gas ring. Brian Ginger remembers "It was a weekly ritual which Arthur insisted we adhered to." The hearth and fireplace were also kept spotless.

B. D. J. WALSH

LEISTON

The signal box and hand-operated level crossing, with the station approach on the right. The buildings at the back were part of Garretts works and often referred to as 'Top Works'. Scotches were located on each side of the level crossing to stop any runaway movements, but were not interlocked with points or signals.

B. D. J. WALSH

DAILY ROUTINES

Ivan Watling started at Leiston as a Junior Goods Clerk in 1943, working with Albert Denny and Cliff Lilley, both of whom had worked at the station since at least the early 1920s, Lilley being related to an earlier Station Master. Both Ivan and Cliff worked from 9.0 am to 5.0 pm and until 1.0 pm on Saturday, but Mr Denny rarely worked on Saturdays. Ivan recalls "I was something of a dogsbody and at 15 rather scared of some of the things that used to happen – I never knew quite what to make of it at times". As an example of this, one of the signalmen was always playing tricks and one day got on the roof of the goods shed office and placed an old slate over the chimney pot. He then entered the office and suggested to Mr Lilley that the fire needed more coal as it "was looking rather poorly". The result can be easily imagined. "I was petrified and didn't know quite what to do but soon saw through the prank when the signalman burst out into fits of laughter".

Ivan dealt with similar work to Thelma at Saxmundham and remembers starting the day by collecting the post from the station and after handing all correspondence to Mr Denny, sorted the invoices which had been sent by the for-

Continued on page 41

J15 class 65467 with an Aldeburgh train at Leiston.

B. D. J. WALSH

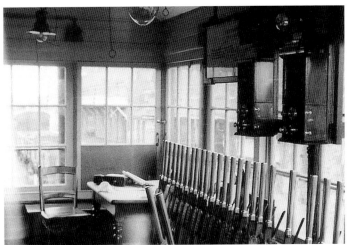

The Saxmundham Junction end of the box. The stove was situated on the left of the chair in the corner and the signalman's locker was behind the chair to the right.

Looking towards the signal box from the station platform. The wagons standing in the loop were probably awaiting collection by the daily goods train.

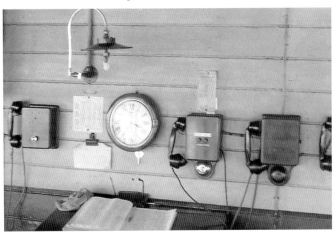

The right and left outer telephones were used for working with the gangers' trolley (left Aldeburgh section, right Saxmundham section). The phone next to the clock was the general line to other boxes, crossing keepers, station masters, booking office, etc. The telephone second from the right was for communication with the shunter in the yard. The open book on the desk was the train register. Note the clock key under the clock, gas lamp, bellcode list over the phone next to the clock, and on the desk Signalman Goddard's glasses and lever duster.

Levers No. 6 and No. 14 are seen here with 'Line blocked' lever collars on them. Lever No. 8 (pulled over with cloth on) was a lock bar on facing points No. 24 and No. 16 facing points had No. 17 lever for the lockbar. Notice the table at bottom left.

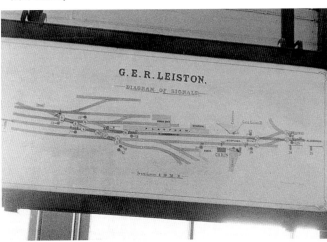

The signal box diagram shows the brickwork siding on the right. The connection to the branch was evidently out of use by the early 1940s and was later removed.

All photos B. D. J. WALSH

The station buildings viewed from the signal box. As with Aldeburgh, in later years the station rooms were not lived in by the Station Master. By the Second World War, Albert Flatt, a permanent way department timekeeper at Saxmundham, and his wife lived there. From left to right, the ground floor rooms were as follows: porters room at the Saxmundham end, lamp room, an archway leading to the gents toilet, followed by the double doors to the booking hall. As at Aldeburgh, doors on the right and left led to the booking office and waiting rooms/ladies toilet. The booking office was also laid out in a similar fashion except that on the platform side there was a partition behind which the Station Master had his desk. There was also a sealed door (as at Aldeburgh) which had at one time led through from the Station Master's house to the booking office.

B. D. J. WALSH

The station building at Leiston was of standard East Suffolk design, of brick construction, it was more or less devoid of decoration, and to Victorian eyes this two-storey, hip-roofed structure would have looked exceedingly plain. Modern travellers, on the other hand, would have been charmed by its classical proportions and the flanking pavilions which (being positioned slightly forward of the main block) provided convenient supports for a miniature platform canopy. Unusually, the adjacent brick-built goods shed was also given a projecting platform canopy, and this feature, was, moreover, much larger than the one on the station building.

B. D. J. WALSH

Leiston Goods Yard, photographed from a Saxmundham-bound train. The lean-to office at the goods shed was the weighbridge office, the new brickwork no doubt being a legacy of the accident described in the text. The weighbridge was used principally for sugar beet traffic. The office had a weighing machine on the shed road side and was equipped with a chair and stove, the chimney of which is visible. Incidentally, Garretts had their own weighbridge and weighed all consignments, even the 'smalls' traffic, themselves. The main goods office was the separate building seen behind the yard crane. A door at the station end, with a window alongside, led into the office, which had a lobby used in part for the storage of paperwork. Another door then led to the main part of the office. The chief clerk sat on the left (branch line side, in front of the window) and the other two clerks on the other side, facing the road approach. A large fireplace was at the yard end. The yard entrance gates were behind the office. A telephone was located in the yard so that the signalman could be contacted when a train was ready to leave or make a shunt on to the branch.

DEREK CLAYTON

The roadside view of the goods shed, with the yard entrance gate on the right. The shed was extended at the station end probably around the time of the Great War and two additional bays were added. There were two small cranes on the shed deck, apparently opposite the bay in the foreground.
B. D. J. WALSH

GOODS TRAFFIC

WARTIME TRAFFIC

In 1943, what were referred to by railway staff as 'Brick Rubble Trains' arrived at Leiston with material salvaged from bomb-damaged areas (mainly London), which was used to build an airfield at Theberton on some 500 acres of land. Ted Barrell remembers working on these trains during his early firing days and recalls that on arrival at Leiston the wagons were shunted to the back road of the goods yard where they were unloaded. The airfield was for the United States 8th Air Force and principally a fighter escort base. The 358th Fighter Group were the first to be based there, being operational from mid-December 1943, their place soon being taken by the 357th Group with P51 Mustang Fighters. The 'Yanks' represented a flamboyant image. Typically they had sweets and ice cream which were unheard of in rationed Great Britain, and Ivan Watling remembers they came in the goods office and distributed these luxuries to the staff. However, one day they blotted their copybook when a train load of supplies arrived and had been left at one of the holding sidings, ready to be gravitated down when the shunter returned from his lunch break. Not being prepared to wait, the Americans decided to move the wagons themselves. They took off sufficient brakes and allowed the trucks to roll, the intention being that they should run into the siding at the back of the yard where the military lorries could reach them. However, the yard points had not been set for this move, and

when the error had been realised, an attempt was made to alter the points, but too late. The leading vehicle was derailed and shunting ceased for the rest of the day. The USAF left the base in July 1945 and from October RAF No 18 Recruit Centre, Technical Training Command were based there for a few years.

Supplies for the USAF were not the only rail-borne military traffic and Leiston became the receiving point for a Central Food Store at Carlton Park, near Saxmundham, serving apparently mainly British bases in the area. The supplies were collected by staff from the store, who were generous in letting the station staff have any spillages or defective consignments. For example, once a sugar bag split and paper was laid on the goods shed floor to collect it and left for the staff – a welcome treat in those austere times.

SUGAR BEET

This traffic was despatched principally by Mr Beecher of Bulls Hall, Knodishall, and it was dealt with in the same way as at Saxmundham. Pamela Strowger (later Smith) recalls the traffic as being very heavy, with several wagons under load in the yard at once during the season.

ANIMALS

John Emsden, a former Leiston butcher, remembers during the postwar meat rationing period (which lasted until 1954), cattle being received from such places as Tavistock, Devon, and

Banbury, Oxfordshire, under government orders. He recalls going to the station and leading the animals from the pens to the slaughterhouse situated behind his shop in Aldeburgh Road. The cattle were driven down Station Road, up Gas Hill and along Cross Street to the traffic lights, and finally along Aldeburgh Road to the slaughter house. Apart from this period the pens saw only occasional use.

COAL

Most of the coal received was for the gas works situated beyond the station at what later became a coal concentration point for Charrington Fuels (which incidentally incorporated Moy who had formerly been at Aldeburgh). Coke and tar were also sent out but destinations have not been established. Domestic coal was dealt with principally by merchants Smith and Coleman. Charles Smith had set up in business sometime between 1904 and 1912, trading from Valley Road, Leiston. By 1922, in addition his son Charles Frederick was in business at Sizewell Road. By the mid-1920s his father had evidently retired and Charles Frederick continued, and by 1937 was trading at Eastward Ho! The business was later run by Herbert Smith from St George's Avenue. Coleman was on the scene later and Robert John Coleman had set up in business at Eastward Ho! by the late 1920s, his son Robert taking over shortly before the Second World War.

Again looking towards Saxmundham, with the starting signal and short-arm signal authorising movements into the sidings. The goods shed road was behind the platform and just visible above the van is the roof of the stables which adjoined the cattle pens. The exchange sidings for Garretts are seen on the left. The 95 mile post represented the distance from Liverpool Street.

B. D. J. WALSH

The Saxmundham end of Leiston viewed from the up starting signal, with the branch on the left and holding sidings on the right. As described in the text, wagons could be gravitated from here into the goods yard as required. However, as can be seen, one siding was normally left clear to enable an Aldeburgh-bound goods train to detach the Aldeburgh portion while dealing with the rest of the train. The concrete permanent way cabin in the foreground replaced a sleeper-built one. The shed in the distance, beyond the buffer stops of the holding sidings, was for the permanent way gang's motorised trolley. The road on the right was nicknamed 'Westward Ho!'.

B. D. J. WALSH

Continued from page 35

warding stations and represented the traffic which was arriving the same day or in the near future. The invoices were sorted and later pasted into a large guard book and given progressive numbers which were cross-referenced with the delivery sheets as a complete record of the receipt and delivery of all consignments.

Ivan spent the middle part of the morning preparing the delivery sheets. This work was carried out on the goods shed deck with Harry Sawyer calling out the various consignments. There were two rounds, the town (on a daily basis) and the country runs; Arthur Cant covered the town every morning and the country with his Scammell lorry during selected afternoons as traffic demanded. Two sets of delivery sheets were prepared, one for each round, and traffic stacked on the shed deck in separate piles according to the area of delivery. As already stated, the Leiston motor driver also assisted at Saxmundham when necessary. The Leiston lorry also delivered and collected parcels traffic which was 'sheeted' by one of the booking clerks. As junior, Ivan was responsible for preparing the paste which arrived from the railway stores in long sticks. This had to be put in boiling water before use. "A very messy job".

Harry Sawyer recorded the numbers of wagons in and out and his record book, which

he kept in the weighbridge office, was consulted by the clerks who maintained their own ledger of all wagons passing through the yard. He also removed the wagon labels from the railway side and kept these in date order in the weighbridge office. When necessary, traders could remove the labels on the other (yard) side which were kept for their records. He also removed one set of labels from the wagons destined for the Gas Works and Sizewell, both of which were under Leiston's control. Incidentally, when train loads or full loads of miltary equipment arrived, the invoices were usually with the wagon label and the porter removed these and handed them in to the goods office. Ivan remembers the amount of paperwork generated was enormous and storage a constant problem, much of it having to be stacked in the lobby of the goods office.

Albert Denny got Ivan involved in other work, particularly the charging of Irish traffic being consigned by Garretts. The well-known local engineers sent a lot of spare parts for farming equipment they had already supplied to Irish farmers. At first, the charging procedure, involving as it did sea charges, etc, was difficult, but "I soon began to enjoy it and it became valuable grounding for my future railway career".

The routine of the office culminated each calendar month in the preparation of the end of period accounts, something for which Mr Denny was personally responsible. After spending a considerable time during the morning trying to balance the books, he placed them in a pile on his chair and, just before going to lunch, struck them with a long ebony ruler, declaring "They'll be right when I come back". Ivan was later made aware that this ritual worked although in reality, of course a break for Mr Denny was enough to stimulate his brain and trace the offending figure! To a young lad it must have all seemed so strange at the time.

All the goods shed staff took their lunch break at the same time and Albert Denny and Cliff Lilley, who both lived in Leiston, went home for lunch. Ivan, who lived in Aldeburgh, stayed put and ate his sandwiches. One day while Ivan was eating his lunch, there was a loud crash from the direction of the weighbridge office at the end of the goods shed. Ivan went outside to find the end wall of the office partly demolished by a wagon. He was immediately concerned about Harry Sawyer who usually ate his lunch in a chair propped up near the damaged wall. "Imagine my relief when he emerged from the station toilets – he was indeed a very lucky man."

Garretts engine Sirapite *dealing with wagons on the loop. The driver was almost certainly Percy Newstead and the shunter 'Jumbo' Brightwell.*
R. C. RILEY/TRANSPORT TREASURY

Pamela Strowger (later Smith) covered the same duties as Ivan in about 1950 and recalls the procedures had changed little, although she also remembered the goods delivery sheets were cross checked with the consignment records to ensure everything had been delivered. This exercise was usually carried out the day after the delivery.

Geoff Smith, who became a booking clerk at Leiston in 1949, remembers "The office routine was fairly standard. I suppose our biggest ticket sales would be cheap day returns to Ipswich. The 'Runabout' tickets in the summer were very popular." At their onset they were priced at ten shillings and lasted a week from Monday to Sunday, with unlimited daily travel on the Eastern Region. The most popular destinations would be Lowestoft, Norwich, Ipswich and Felixstowe. "I did early and late shift, the first train being just after 7.0 a.m. and the last around 9.0 p.m. In the summer I worked every other Sunday."

The signalmen worked similar hours to their colleagues at Saxmundham Junction, the overlap being used in the same way. Brian Ginger, one of the signalmen in the late 1950s, recalls the early-turn Saturday returned as late-turn Monday, with the Saturday late-turn man working on Sunday when required. Each man therefore had a long weekend off every other week.

Garretts' shunting loco Sirapite *working in the private sidings. She was built by Aveling and Porter in 1906 and originally owned by Gypsum Mines Ltd., Mountfield, Sussex. Garretts appear to have purchased the loco during the 1930s, prior to which horses had been used. In the final years,* Sirapite *was not in regular use and a small battery loco dealt with the shunting. The driver was a well-known figure, Percy Newstead, and the man on the left was 'Jumbo' Brightwell, who also worked for Garretts and covered the shunting duties. The man on the right has not been identified. The picture provides a further glimpse of the stables and cattle pens. The stables were for two horses and there was a dung compound at the station end. The coal wharves are apparent behind. During the 1940s, Herbert Smith had wharves in the yard, but the other merchant, Coleman, bagged supplies direct from the wagons.*
B. D. J. WALSH

By the late 1950s, Harry Sawyer assisted on the platform as well as undertaking his goods yard duties. By this time, Sid Skippings was covering the morning trains and travelled in from Ipswich on the first DMU, with Harry coming on duty later in the morning to cover the goods yard work and shunting, after which he relieved Sid and manned the station until the early evening. Harry is remembered as a very meticulous and methodical man who would not be rushed. One of his hobbies was mountain climbing and he is said to have scaled many peaks in Scotland and Wales.

Geoff Smith, who incidentally also later worked at Garretts, recalls the Pye traffic. "It was common practice for them to bring loads of radio sets for despatch at the end of the working day to catch the 5.0 p.m. out. It was usually a last minute thing with recording taking place as they were loaded into the guard's compartment."

Geoff also remembers "Pigeons for racing were a regular source of traffic. The Leiston and Aldeburgh pigeon clubs were very strong. There was a specific way of charging which included the return of the empty baskets."

A general view from the platform towards Thorpeness, with the goods shed on the left and the signal box and level crossing in the distance. The wagons on the loop were probably awaiting collection by the branch goods. Garretts sidings are seen on the right with an overhead gantry crane to unload raw materials and load large outward consignments. This crane appears to have been the 30 ton appliance referred to in official documents and may have been installed during the 1920s. Reference has also been traced to an earlier 15 ton crane but whether this was on the same site is unclear. The line curving away to the right went to the 'Top Works'. The line to 'Bottom Works' can be seen passing between the right-hand leg of the crane and the bush. A siding existed beyond the level crossing on the down side and this had earlier served a brick works owned by W. H. Carr (later Carr and Co.). The siding appears to have been in use from at least the early 1890s until the 1920s and is shown on the signal box diagram on page 36. The Gas Works Siding further down the line was approved in August 1912.

A closer view of the crane. Incidentally, authority was given for a crane in June 1893 at an estimated cost of £480, but whether this work actually took place and whether it was the earlier crane, mentioned in the previous caption, is unclear.
COLLECTION R. K. BLENCOWE

Sirapite at work within the lower part of the Garrett complex on 14th May 1956.   H. C. CASSERLEY

RICHARD GARRETT LTD (SUBSIDIARY OF BEYER PEACOCK)

Garretts, with their private sidings, generated the most lucrative business for the railway and, although full loads of machinery were exchanged with their factory, there were also heavy flows of 'smalls' traffic, mostly, as already mentioned, spare parts for machinery. This traffic was so substantial that the motor lorry called at the factory every day to pick up consignments. Apart from inwards traffic, full loads of steel offcuts were despatched in open trucks, principally to Sheffield for smelting. Coal arrived for the Power House at the 'Top Works' (nearest the station) and the Foundry at the 'Bottom Works', which was reached via the rail link from the station. Bill Lucerne was the Transport Manager at Garretts and ordered wagons from the goods office. One customer remembered was Bord na Mona, a peat company in Ireland, who purchased peat-digging equipment.

Geoff Smith remembers "These were ungainly machines with a large, wide seed wheel at each corner to negotiate the Irish peat bogs. They were painted a bright yellow. My father worked in Garretts and had spoken of these machines being finished painting right up to the very last minute – in fact the painters would still be working on them right up to the time of loading – it has been said that painters even went to Saxmundham station to put the last touches on!"

Bob Wisby worked for Garretts during the early postwar years, mainly on security gate work at Station Road and Main Street. At this time traffic was being exchanged with the railway at both parts of the works but by the late 1950s Brian Ginger remembers only the connections at the signal box end being used and traffic exchanged for unloading by the overhead crane (behind the signal box) or transfer to the Bottom Works. As far as the early postwar years were concerned, the main traffics were foundry coke, coal, steel in plates and pig iron. Most of the coal was destined for the boiler house at Bottom Works and foundry coke for the foundry connected to the private sidings along the route between the two works. Machinery manufactured was usually loaded at the Top Works using the overhead crane. Oil tanks arrived occasionally for the plating shop. Even by this period, parts of the Top Works were being let out to other firms, *viz* S. & S. Corrugated Manufacturing Co, who produced corrugated cardboard, and Pye Radios who regularly despatched large quantities of parcels on the 4.55 pm Aldeburgh to Saxmundham train.

Geoff Smith remembers "Much of the traffic would be in wagon loads – steel plates for the boiler shop situated at the bottom of the yard and backing on to Goss Street." By the mid-1950s some of the foundry coke was arriving by road but pig-iron was evidently still railborne. Locomotive chassis were built in the erecting shop in the top works and despatched on low loader rail wagons to Garrett's parent company which at the time was Beyer Peacock of Manchester.

WORKING BETWEEN TOP AND BOTTOM WORKS

The works locomotive *Sirapite* was used to sort wagons and, although not apparently permitted onto the branch, it was able to exchange wagons at sidings alongside the station where wagons were left or collected. When movements were made to and from the Works, in addition to the Driver, Percy Newstead, the locomotive was accompanied by a shunter, 'Jumbo' Brightwell who, along with the gateman from the Top Works or the Bottom Works, flagged the train across Station Road and Main Street respectively.

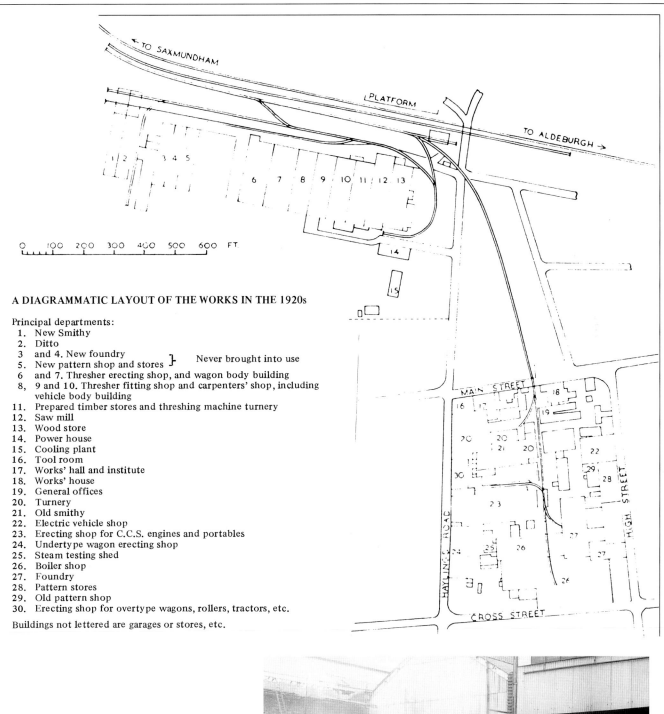

A DIAGRAMMATIC LAYOUT OF THE WORKS IN THE 1920s

Principal departments:
1. New Smithy
2. Ditto
3. and 4. New foundry
5. New pattern shop and stores } Never brought into use
6. and 7. Thresher erecting shop, and wagon body building
8, 9 and 10. Thresher fitting shop and carpenters' shop, including vehicle body building
11. Prepared timber stores and threshing machine turnery
12. Saw mill
13. Wood store
14. Power house
15. Cooling plant
16. Tool room
17. Works' hall and institute
18. Works' house
19. General offices
20. Turnery
21. Old smithy
22. Electric vehicle shop
23. Erecting shop for C.C.S. engines and portables
24. Undertype wagon erecting shop
25. Steam testing shed
26. Boiler shop
27. Foundry
28. Pattern stores
29. Old pattern shop
30. Erecting shop for overtype wagons, rollers, tractors, etc.

Buildings not lettered are garages or stores, etc.

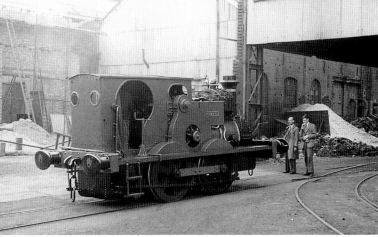

A closer view of Sirapite, *again within the confines of the works area, again on 14th May 1956.* H. C. CASSERLEY

To be continued

CORRESPONDENCE

Mr. T. R. Perkins — track-basher extraordinary

In his article in BRJ No. 74, R. Tourret wonders if anyone knows what the 'T.R.' stood for. The answer is Thomas Richard, as evidenced from the tribute to him in the *SLS Journal* for January 1953.

Brian Lacey
East Grinstead

Reading South

What a comprehensive article and such excellent photographs. What you do not mention, though, is that the double line spur between Reading Junction Box and the Great Western station was built, owned and maintained by the London & South Western Railway who had a small detached P-way gang stationed at Reading to look after it. Presumably it was built to facilitate LSWR goods traffic passing between London and the GWR, and coal traffic passing the other way.

Now I had not really thought about it before this article, but from the photograph of Reading Junction Box it is obviously an LSWR structure, and as such would have been maintained by that railway's staff as part of the same department as the P-way gang. Does anyone know if the signalmen were also South Western men? It seems logical that they should have been, but rather unusual if that were the case to work with South Eastern men on both sides. If this was indeed the situation, I would guess the SE&CR Block Regulations were used, but it would be interesting to know.

As a signalman on the Windsor lines many years ago, one remembers that the Reading trains were very definitely top of the pecking order so to speak. Their time-keeping was very good and anyone who delayed a Reading could definitely expect a 'Please explain'. At Feltham East, one put a freight out behind most Down Readings and, on the Up, one came in just in front of the Up Reading, it went without saying that one ensured the Up freights had a clear run into the yard.

One day, Control rang up asking rather unnecessarily that a certain Eastleigh freight be given a clear run into the yard. I asked what was so special about this particular train and was told "You will see". Came the time and in came a Brighton K class locomotive on the front of 65 and only a minute or two down. It transpired that Feltham's S15 had failed at Eastleigh and all they had there as a replacement for the return trip was this K fresh out of shops. The crew knew nothing of the engine's brake and had, by all accounts, brought the train all the way from Eastleigh using nothing but the tender hand brake.

Feltham men apparently hated all things 'Brighton' and I remember one day two young drivers were having a 'pushing competition' between two SECR class Cs recently arrived, displaced from Hither Green. "Look at them", said an old driver who happened to be in the box, "f.....g useless Brighton engines", apparently mistaking the Stirling steam reverser for a Westinghouse pump!

One last 'Brighton' story. We used to have a heavy freight down from Nine Elms in the early hours, normally hauled by a Urie H16 tank. This train, rather than enter the yard at the Junction end, would come down the main and then proceed to knock off its train in several cuts from the main line., the bulk of it to form the 04.30 to Reading — quite a performance I might say. Something to make a modern H&S man curl up and die! One morning, it was 'warned on' from Feltham Junction but it then proceeded to take a very long time in section. When at last it struggled into sight, it was seen to be headed by a Brighton E6 0−6−2T, a class probably never seen before at Feltham. Anyway, it was clearly in trouble, so I opened the window to hear what the driver had to say, which was not much − "Get the 3.50 to pull me in." So that was done, but it completely mucked up the yard's usual arrangements for dealing with the train. Now I know that on their home ground these E6s were capable of doing useful work, but this one was clearly past it and whoever thought it could do the job of an H16 must have been living on another planet; perhaps they did not know of the nature of the shunting involved on arrival. It was said at the time that this engine was intended to become the Feltham shed pilot and that someone had thought this was a good way of delivering it. Whatever, I never set eyes on it again and, looking back, I am inclined to think it was on its way to Eastleigh for scrapping.

Alan Blackburn
Woking

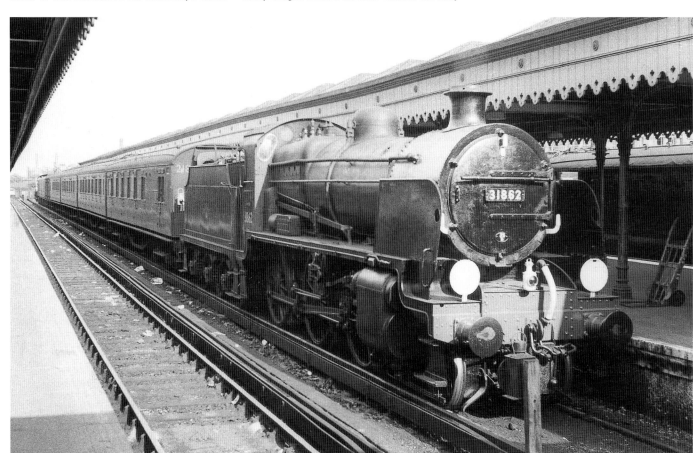

P. Q. Treloar kindly submitted this picture of No. 31862 at Reading South in the late 1950s.

The Tylwch Accident
and the 'Signalling of Trains at Crossing Places'
by MIKE CHRISTENSEN

Tylwch, circa — well, the dating is interesting. This photograph appears to show the then-new signalling and (to the right in this view) the down platform as commissioned in June 1899. But the locomotive was No. 23, an 0–4–2 tender loco built by Kitson & Co. of Leeds in 1864, their works number 1239, and acquired by the Cambrian Railways from the Mid Wales Railway (their No. 3) on 2nd April 1888 (when the Cambrian took over the operation of the MWR). This locomotive was withdrawn in December 1896, more than two years before the altered arrangements bringing the down platform into use. The platform had been shown on plans for the new layout in 1891, but should not have been used for passenger trains since the line that served it was only a siding, with no point locks on the trap points. Yet the platform on which the men stood had all the appearance of being laid out for, and used by, passengers. Why else would there be a pair of bench seats and neat gardens? And three of the men on the platform appear to be workmen painting and tidying up. This was probably a posed view, so the signalman had placed the down home signal (lever 2) to danger to protect the train, even though the rear of the train was still foul of the points protected by the signal. The very barren countryside in this area is amply demonstrated in this view from C. C. Green's collection.

The station at Tylwch on the Mid-Wales Railway opened on 21st September 1864, at the time of the opening of the line. It was a small, remote stopping place serving a population in the immediate vicinity of just 32 people, but also a wider area connected by a narrow road. The station was situated on the steep climb of the Mid-Wales line out of the valley of the River Severn to a summit just north of Pantydwr, from where the line descended equally steeply to the valley of the River Wye. From Llanidloes to Tylwch the climb included over a mile at 1 in 75, $\frac{3}{4}$ mile at 1 in 60 and $\frac{1}{2}$ mile at 1 in 104. The gradient eased for a short distance at 1 in 530 through Tylwch station before the climb was resumed with $1\frac{1}{4}$ miles at 1 in 111. Continuing southwards to the summit, the climb was at 1 in 85 for

$\frac{3}{4}$ mile, then finally $1\frac{1}{2}$ mile at 1 in 77. The distance from Pantydwr to Tylwch was 3 miles 74 chains, falling sharply all the way and losing some 200 feet in height.

Various strands of history came together at Tylwch on Saturday 16th September 1899. James Davies, the station master, (aged 33) came on duty at 5.00 am. He had been at Tylwch since 13th January, having previously worked in the role of clerk at Welshpool, Oswestry and Newtown. At Newtown he had learned to work the Train Tablet instruments, and along the way he must have learned the signalling regulations. He expected to be busy early that day because the first train of the day, the Down Mail (5.30 am Moat Lane Junction to Brecon) was to cross an excursion from Builth Wells to Manchester. The excursion

was to leave Builth Wells at 5.10 am, but it was delayed by loading passengers and adding a coach at Rhayader (there was a 'large number' of passengers here), so the train was some 17 minutes late when Pantydwr asked for the release for a tablet at 5.50. The Down Mail, due off Moat Lane at 5.30, was about sixteen minutes late. Llanidloes asked 'Is Line Clear' for a tablet at 6.02. The 'Train entering section' bell signal was given by Llanidloes at 6.09 and by Pantydwr for the excursion train half a minute later.

The Down Mail whistled for the signals first – at about 6.14 – so Davies set the road by reversing 9 (up facing points), locking the down facing points by pulling 6, and clearing the home signal 2. Somewhere in his training, Davies had been taught the

A close-up view of the accident scene, taken from the road overbridge at the south end of the crossing loop. The six-wheel van No. 6 (which was immediately behind the engine of the excursion train) had ridden up over the frame of the following bogie composite coach No. 266, and demolished the carriage sides and partitions to nearly half the length of the coach. It was in the third compartment of coach 266 that the fatally injured passenger was travelling. Davies told the enquiry that when he reached Margaret Rowlands, she was completely buried in wreckage, 'just alive and nothing more'. Another man and a woman were also in that third compartment. The man had his face and leg injured, but the woman was unhurt. Looking at the damage, she must have counted herself lucky indeed. Six workmen who were (improperly) travelling in the six-wheel van No. 6 were also lucky to be uninjured. The signal in this photograph was the Down Starting signal No. 3. The problem of a vehicle riding up over the headstock of another, and the resulting telescoping of the two vehicles, was a significant problem in the era of coaching stock of timber construction and screw couplings. It was recog-

nised in a Cambrian Railways instruction. The 1911 Appendix stated: 'Passengers must not be allowed, under any circumstances whatever, to travel in the compartment next to the engine. Guards will be held responsible for seeing that the compartments in question are empty, and the doors locked before their trains start, and that the doors are kept locked during the journey. District Inspectors and Station Masters are required to take care that this regulation is strictly observed.' C. C. Green noted that the two photographs of the accident were copied from prints owned by Stephen Humphries. Just who took the photos is uncertain, but the photographer must have been on the scene within 90 minutes of the accident to manage to photograph the damaged coaches before they were moved. It seems possible that he was alerted to the event by Cambrian officials and that he travelled up from Llanidloes with the breakdown vans called hurriedly to assist. Stationmaster Davies sent a message by phonopore (an early version of telephone) 'at once' when the accident happened — a train 'with doctors and assistance' arrived at 7.0 a.m.

A more distant view of the accident scene. The two badly damaged vehicles of the excursion train, still locked together, had been drawn in to the down platform, to allow the rest of the Manchester excursion train to proceed on its journey. The extent of the damage to coach No. 266 (a relatively new vehicle, built by Ashbury) is amply apparent. The six-wheeled van had pushed into the coach until the first set of axleguards on the van came up against the buffer beam headstock of the coach. It was fortunate that there was a second-class compartment in the coach, which was empty. Of the other coaches in the excursion train, No. 204 (which was next to 266) suffered a broken headstock, together with bent buffer rods and step irons. The next six vehicles were undamaged, but the tenth vehicle (four-wheeled third-class coach No. 39) had a headstock damaged. Shock forces in accidents can act in curious ways. The Down Mail train was stationary when the collision happened. Yet the list of damage to that train as it was violently pushed back 19 yards was extensive (although none of the twelve passengers on the train were hurt): Engine No. 65 — Steel buffer beam badly bent and angle irons broken; frames and life guards badly bent and splashers damaged; footplate and fall plates damaged; flexible vacuum pipes destroyed and wrought iron vacuum pipes damaged, bogie slightly damaged. Cambrian third class coach No. 158 — One broken headstock, two buffer castings and one stay rod broken; two buffer rods bent. Cambrian composite coach No. 149 — One headstock, two headstock caps, three buffer castings, two buffer blocks, one footboard and two step irons all broken. Cambrian third class coach No. 241 — One headstock, one buffer casting and one step stay broken; and mouldings at ends and sides damaged. Cambrian passenger van No. 104 was the only vehicle in this (short) train undamaged.

need to set the far end points for the same line that the train was arriving on, though the locking at Tylwch did not require this. As the Mail slowed to a halt in the down platform, Davies took the tablet from the driver and checked the tickets for the few passengers who had alighted. He then crossed to the up side platform at the south end of the station, intending to go to the station office to clear the tablet and get 'Line Clear' from Llanidloes for the excursion before proceeding to the signalbox at the north end of the station to reset the signals and points. As he got on to the up platform, he heard the driver of the excursion train whistle urgently.

The driver of the Up Excursion was Samuel Hopkins, aged 40 and a regular driver for only the last three months. He had gone on duty at 4.20 am to take charge of engine No. 49 (an 0–6–0 with four-wheeled tender) and make up his train, which was initially of 10 vehicles (two brake vans and eight coaches). Approaching Tylwch station, he could not stop his train, which over-ran the up home signal. In the ordinary way Hopkins would have had an overlap of a few hundred yards beyond the signal in which to regain control of his train. But No 9 points were still set towards the down platform, as they had been when the Down Mail train arrived. Fireman Stephen Humphreys of the Down Mail was alerted to the emergency by Hopkins' frantic whistling, and as he stepped from the footplate on to the platform, called to his driver that the excursion train was about to collide with the Mail. His driver,

Richard Jones, was still trying to release the brake and get his locomotive into reverse, to reduce the impact, when the collision occurred at about 6.17 am. His engine and train were forced back some 19 yards. The two locomotives met buffer to buffer at a speed which Hopkins estimated at five miles per hour – but which was clearly greater than this. The coaches behind excursion train locomotive No 49 tele-scoped, the frame of the six-wheel van No. 6 (immediately behind the engine) riding up over that of the bogie composite coach No. 266 behind it (the coach which had been added at Rhayader). A woman trav-elling in the third compartment of coach 266 was killed, and seven other people in the excursion train were injured, though their injuries were stated not to be serious – they were 'cut and bruised'.

The excursion train, minus vehicles 6 and 266, was dispatched forward to Man-chester at 7.32 am with an engine that had arrived from Llanidloes. Two vehicles were put off later, third class coach No. 204 at Llanidloes, and third class coach No. 39 at Moat Lane, because of the damage which it was discovered they had sustained. A second up excursion passed through Tylwch at 8.02, and the Down Mail proceeded, hauled by another locomotive, at 9.00 am.

In the report of his enquiry for the Board of Trade (BoT) – published on 6th October 1899 – Lt. Col. H. A. Yorke noted that Driver Hopkins of the excursion train explained his inability to control the train by the fact that the vacuum brake was not working properly and that he had only been

able to obtain 14 inches of vacuum. Yorke did not accept this explanation. The driver who had used the engine the previous day had experienced no problems. The driver of No. 10 (which was summoned to remove the remaining coaches of excursion and work them forward to Manchester) had no problem in obtaining and maintaining 22 inches of vacuum. The train had aver-aged 30 miles per hour in the section from Pantydwr to Tylwch, so whilst Hopkins was not speeding to make up for lost time, he was certainly not proceeding cautiously, as might be expected from a driver who believed that his brakes might be defective (or at least weak). Yorke held Hopkins primarily responsible for the accident. He concluded that Hopkins had expected that since his train was 17 minutes late the Mail would have long since arrived at Tylwch, so that the home signal would be cleared for him when he arrived there. Unfor-tunately it was not, and when Hopkins first sighted the home signal at 'danger' at a distance of some 599 yards from the signal, it was too late for his braking to stop the train (it was drizzling with rain at the time) before the signal. It was the more unfor-tunate that the points were set so as to deprive Hopkins of the safety overlap he might have expected. The locomotive of the Down Mail train was standing just 97 yards beyond the up home signal (12).

As regards the working at the station, Yorke commented that whilst one man could clearly handle the passage of the early-morning Mail train on his own, two men ought to be on duty when trains were

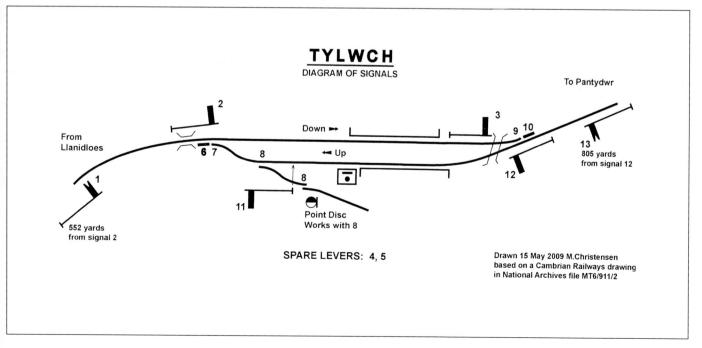

TYLWCH

DIAGRAM OF SIGNALS

To Pantydwr

From Llanidloes

Down ➡

⬅ Up

2

3

9 10

13
805 yards
from signal 12

6 7

8

8

12

1

11

Point Disc
Works with 8

552 yards
from signal 2

SPARE LEVERS: 4, 5

Drawn 15 May 2009 M.Christensen
based on a Cambrian Railways drawing
in National Archives file MT6/911/2

to be crossed. Yorke chastised station master Davies for having cleared the home signal before the Mail train had completely stopped at it, though this had nothing at all to do with the collision. We may sympathise with Davies here. The wording of the relevant part of the Cambrian Railways Appendix to the Working Time Book as from 15th June 1888 was:

'Signalling of Trains at Crossing Places. When two trains are arranged to meet at any Train Staff or Block Station on the single line, all the signals must be kept at 'Danger' against both trains, and the proper distant signal lowered for the train that whistles first, the signal in the opposite direction being kept at danger until the train for which the other has been lowered has come to a stand in the station. When the train is at perfect rest, the signal against the train coming in the opposite direction may then be lowered.'

This had been changed, however, and the more restrictive wording of the Cambrian Railways Rule book from 1894 was:

'When trains which have to cross each other are approaching a Tablet or Staff Station in opposite directions, the signals in both directions must be kept at Danger; and when the first train has been brought to a stand the Home Signal applicable to such train may be lowered to allow it to draw forward to the Station or Starting Signal; and after it has come to a stand and the signalman has seen that the line on which the other train will arrive is quite clear, the necessary signals for that train may also be lowered.'

But Davies knew that the trains were late, that both trains were going to arrive at pretty much the same time, and that if he brought the Mail to a complete stand, the driver would have to restart his train on a rising gradient of 1 in 104 on a wet rail.

Yorke also commented, with some justification, that Davies 'had taken little pains to acquaint himself with the signalling', which after all had been completely changed only months before to conform with the then 'modern practice'. Davies had been stationmaster at the station at the time when these changes had been made. But when Yorke roundly criticised stationmaster Davies 'who for some reason had got it into his head that it was necessary to pull over No. 9 lever, and so set the points at the south end of the loop for the Down Road before lowering the (home) signal, and accordingly did so', he was arguably being less than fair. Davies had not simply 'got it into his head' that the points at the south end of the loop needed to be set for the down line before the Down Mail could be admitted to the platform. Somewhere in his training he had been

taught to do this. And that learning had its origins in Board of Trade requirements of less than ten years before.

The Regulation of Railways Act 1889 (RRA89) required that points and signals be interlocked on lines of railway open to passengers. This had been a requirement for new work since recommendations on the subject has been issued in 1860, but the requirement was now applied to all existing railway works as well. The Cambrian Railways, on which few stations or sidings were interlocked at the beginning of 1889 (in a later report to the BoT the company stated that only two stations had been interlocked before the work started!), had a lot of work to do and incurred considerable costs to fulfill the Order formally served on it under the Act on 20th November 1890. The work of interlocking points and signals was not completed within the two years stipulated in the Order.

The expense was made all the greater by a requirement of the BoT that 'Facing points to be avoided as far as possible, but where they cannot be dispensed with, they must be placed as near as practicable to the levers by which they are worked or bolted. The limit of distance from levers working points to be 180 yards in the case of facing points, and 300 yards in the case of trailing points on the main line, or safety points of sidings' (paragraph 5 of the Requirements of the BoT as issued in 1898). This restricted the length of a crossing loop operated by one signal box to an absolute maximum of 360 yards. The distance from the clearing point at one end to the clearing point at the other was considerably less. At Tylwch the distance from facing points to facing points was just 260 yards. The starting signal (at the exit from the loop line) could be no further forward than the clearing point where the two lines converged. The home signal, admitting the train in to the loop, had to be close enough to the entry facing points for the facing point lock bar to be held by a train as soon as the locomotive passed the signal. At Tylwch, for example, the up home signal (12) was just 19 yards from switch blades of 9 points. This requirement meant that the distance from the home signal to the starting signal would always be less than 400 yards.

This was significant in connection with another BoT requirement, the enforcement of block working. In an attempt to obtain uniformity between the various railway companies, the Railway Clearing

House (RCH) Superintendents' Committee agreed standard signalling regulations (RAIL 1080/567). Regulation 4 prescribed that on double lines of railway a train was not to be accepted from the signal box in rear unless the line was clear for at least 440 yards ahead of the home signal, 'and all necessary points within this distance have been placed in their proper position for the safety of the approaching train'. Once a train had been accepted under Regulation 4, no obstruction of the line was to be permitted within the 440 yard safety overlap until the train had either been brought to a stand at the home signal, or the train had passed clear of any connections within the 440 yards up to the acceptance 'clearing point'.

Clearly, the application of Regulation 4 at any short crossing loop would mean that two trains could not be accepted from signalboxes at both sides at the same time. One train would have to arrive in the station before the second could even be accepted in to the section in the other direction. The resultant delays to traffic would be unacceptable.

Another signalling Regulation was available, Regulation 5. Widely known as the 'Warning Arrangement', this allowed a train to be accepted where the block section was clear, but the station or junction beyond the home signal (and within the 440 yards normal overlap) was blocked. The driver of any train accepted under the Warning Arrangement had to be specifically advised of the fact that he did not have any safety overlap, and to proceed therefore with all appropriate caution. Since this otherwise very convenient regulation effectively reduced the safety overlap to all but nothing, it was only authorised in special circumstances, and its use for passenger trains in recent times would been regarded as exceptional.

At a number of its stations, the Cambrian Railways opted to have two signalling installations at the crossing loop. At the larger stations, such as Barmouth, Portmadoc, Llanidloes, Builth Road, and Towyn, there were two cabins each controlling signals, the box at the remote end of the loop often being quite a small affair, just working the loop points and three signals. At smaller stations, such as Abermule, Caersws, Carno, Cemmes Road, Bow Street, Pensarn, and Builth Wells, there was one signalbox, the points at the end of the crossing loop remote from the box being operated from a ground frame (controlled from the signalbox through a lever[s] driving rodding that operated a mechanical lock). An attempt was made by the Cambrian to have a long passing loop at Montgomery with points worked 'on the ground' and simply locked by the wire running to the home signals. The work was ready for inspection by 11th August 1889. Col. Rich, who conducted the inspection for the BoT, would have none of this, and refused permission for the use of the layout. The Cambrian had to rebuild it, bringing the points at the Abermule end of the station within the 180 yard limit and working them from the signalbox, and working the points at the Forden end of the station from a new ground frame, locked by midway bolt from the signalbox. Col. Rich approved this altered layout when he re-inspected Montgomery on 14th March 1891 (MT6/545/10).

It may be noted in passing that having two signal boxes at a station in itself created a problem. This was because there was another BoT expectation, which was that two trains must not be allowed to *enter* the crossing loop (as distinct to approaching it from the adjacent signalbox) at the same time. Where there were two signalboxes, each independently working points and signals, there had to be some interlocking between them. This was achieved at Builth Road, for example, by arranging that the facing point lock for a train to enter the loop in one direction was locked against the slot on the home signal for entry into the loop in the other direction.

This still left a problem at the stations where the loop was short, and the provision of even a ground frame to work the remote points was not necessary. The convention was that Regulation 4 could not be used to accept trains from adjacent signalboxes simultaneously if the full 440 yard overlap was not available to both trains, and that the only method of working the trains would be to apply Regulation 5.

The use of Regulation 5 featured in correspondence between the Cambrian Railways and the BoT which started on 29th October 1886. The Cambrian wrote to ask whether the BoT would sanction a change to substitute working by Electric Train Tablet for the existing methods of working. The BoT raised no objection in principle. On 5th January 1887, the company sent in a copy of its proposed signalling regulations. (It is of interest that this was in the form of a poster-sized sheet, similar to that sent to

the BoT by a number of other companies that were adopting tablet working at this time. It would seem possible, but is not certain, that Tyer & Co provided a draft form of wording.) The BoT was concerned at the suggestion that Regulation 5 would be used whenever trains – passenger trains included – were approaching a station at which they would have to cross. If the Company proposed that all trains should be accepted under the Warning Arrangement when approaching a crossing station at which a crossing was to be made, the position should be clarified.

The Cambrian's response, in a letter dated 15th January 1887, was that if there was an actual obstruction of the line, Regulation 5 would not be allowed to be used, and that special instructions would be given to the driver by the Red Cap pilotman who had the train in his charge. A revised set of proposed regulations sent to the BoT heightened the Inspector's concerns. Col. F. A. Marindin pointed out that, as worded, the revised instructions made matters worse, since they authorised a signalman to obstruct the line as far as his home signal (but not outside it) after accepting a train. This would 'leave only the thickness of the signal post as a margin of safety' (MT6/566/10).

The company sent in another draft set of regulations on 10th February 1887. In a rather weary tone, Marindin noted that the revised regulations contained 'clumsy' wording, but that since they achieved the desired objective, no further objection should be raised.

The Cambrian Railways Appendix to the Working Time Book as from 15th June 1888 contained the following in relation to signalling trains by the Train Tablet System

11. Giving permission for a train to approach, and giving the arrival signal.
      In the case of a non-stopping train, the line must be considered clear, and the Arrival signal be given, immediately the last vehicle (with the tail lamp attached) has passed into the onward section, and the Train Tablet instrument must then be put into its Normal condition, the Train Tablet being deposited in the Cylinder of the Instrument lettered side downwards. In the case of a stopping train, permission must not be given while it remains at the station for another train to approach until the signal 'Section Clear but Station or Junction Blocked' has been given to and acknowledged by the signalman in rear, as provided in Clause 16. After permission has been given for a train to approach, no obstruction of the line on which the train requires to run must be allowed outside the Home Signal, or between the Home and Starting signals.

16. Section Clear but Station or Junction blocked.
      When the line is clear to the Home Signal and it is necessary for a train to be allowed to approach a post cautiously in consequence of an obstruction existing ahead of a Home Signal, or from any other cause, the Train Tablet signal must not be acknowledged, but the bell signal 'Section clear but station or junction blocked' (thirteen beats on the bell, 3–5–5) must be given, and not until this signal has been acknowledged by being repeated must permission be given to the station or signalbox in rear for a Train Tablet to be issued. The signalman receiving the signal 'Section clear but station or junction blocked' must hand the tablet to the driver and verbally instruct him to proceed cautiously to the post from which the signal has been received.

So the Cambrian Railways regulations for Tablet working from 1888 allowed

a) the acceptance of a train provided that the line was clear to the Home Signal and beyond that to the Starting Signal (any preceding train having proceeded on its way).
b) the acceptance of a train if the line was clear to the Home signal but not beyond, but only on the basis that the driver was verbally warned that he had no safety overlap.

The Cambrian Railways' 'clumsy' form of wording was later replaced by the RCH version of Regulation 4 for Signalling on Single Lines. The relevant extract read:

4. Line clear or giving permission for a train to approach
a) Except where instructions are issued to the contrary, the line must not be considered clear, nor must a train be allowed to approach from a token station in rear . . . until all the necessary points have been placed in their proper position for the safety of the approaching train and the line is clear
i) At a Crossing Place, if the line on which the approaching train has to run is clear to the starting signal and the facing points are set for that line.

When the Cambrian Railways decided to adopt tablet working widely across its system, as part of the RRA89 work, it decided that the warning would be achieved by the driver being given a written note of the warning on a card, not simply a verbal warning. In a letter to the BoT (dealing with RRA89 issues) on 3rd October 1893, the company reported that Regulation 5 tickets had now been adopted and that warning cards were being printed (MT6/2079).

So by 1888 the BoT had accepted that it was sufficient for the regulations to require that the line be clear for an overlap beyond the home signal as far at the starting signal (whether that overlap be 440 yards or less, no distance being specified) before a train could be accepted, without any Warning Arrangement. When inspecting new signalling installations, however, the Inspecting Officers were still requiring that at short passing loops the points beyond the starting signal were set for the direction of the incoming train (to create a 440 yard overlap). When Marindin inspected the new signalling at Bow Street in October 1891, for example, he required that 'the levers for the points at one end of the loop should precede the home signal at the other end' (MT6/558/13).

Tylwch was first provided with interlocked signalling (as required by RRA89) on 21st December 1891, when a new signalbox was provided at a cost of £593–6s.-3d. The layout as inspected for the BoT on 19th February 1892, comprised a single line through a passenger platform, with a goods loop siding on the down side of the line (opposite the passenger platform) and a goods siding on the up side. Lt. Col. Yorke (an Inspecting Officer for the BoT from 1891 to 1913) approved the works. There was a platform beside the goods loop siding, in readiness perhaps for the time when the goods loop siding would be converted into a passing loop (MT6/574/9).

Some eight years later it was decided to undertake the upgrading of the goods loop siding into a passing loop to allow the crossing of passenger trains. The work was completed on Sunday 6th June 1899 to the diagram shown on page 49, and inspected by Yorke, for the BoT, on 24th June. Some years having passed since the debates that followed the 1889 Act, the (arguably rather dangerous) requirement that the points at the exit end of the loop should precede the home signal at the entry to the loop no longer existed. It was not included in the locking table for the interlocking. But stationmaster Davies did not know this. It was to be his downfall on that fateful day, just three months after the new signalling was introduced.

At the conclusion of his report, Lt. Col. Yorke delivered a balanced view in the actions of Davies,

'It was a very unfortunate circumstance that the loop points at the south end of the place were set for the down line, and stationmaster Davies committed a most serious mistake in placing them in that position. He says that he thought it was necessary for him to do so before he could lower the down home signal; which shows that he had taken little pains to make himself acquainted with the signalling of the place. It may, however, be stated on his behalf that in former days it was very usual to interlock the points and signals at passing loops on single line in the manner described by Davies. The arrangement had obvious disadvantages which are vividly exemplified in this case. The modern and far preferable practice is for the home signal at either end of the passing loop to be altogether independent of the position of the points at the other end of the loop, as was the case at Tylwch, which had been resignalled and interlocked a few months ago.'

This was probably as close as an Inspecting Officer could go in admitting that the BoT requirements of ten years earlier had been unsafe. Interlocking that required the outgoing loop points reversed to admit a train into the loop had once been routinely required, but had been condemned by Major-General C.S. Hutchinson at Orbliston on the Highland Railway in 1893 (which prompted the Highland to re-lock the signalling at all its crossing loops affected). The reality was that Inspecting Officers of the BoT had held contradictory views on the question. It is a debate that has continued down to the present day.

In practice, the use of Regulation 5 was not common on the Cambrian Railways. The Appendix for 1911 makes no reference to the use of Warning Tickets. The instructions envisaged a verbal warning to the driver, reinforced by the signalman displaying a green (for caution) hand signal. In relation to hand signals, older members of railway staff would remember being taught the catechism 'White is right, red is wrong, and green means gently go along' – and it still applies.

The question of whether it was necessary to use the Regulation 5 Warning Arrangement' when trains were to cross was to come up again even in the 20th century. In 1903, the Caledonian Railway installed a 'break-section' intermediate crossing loop at Glencruitten summit, between Oban and Connel Ferry. This summit is approached by gradients of 1 in 50 in each direction. So the company wanted to be able not only to accept trains in both directions at the same time, but also to be able to admit two trains in to the loop simultaneously – not stopping either at the home signal on a 1 in 50 gradient. To provide for this to be done safely, each loop line was provided both with catch points to prevent any runaways should the rear of the train break free, and also facing traps at the outgoing end of the loop, so that if a train overran the starting signal it would end up in a sand drag, not passing out on to the single line and potentially into collision. The BoT insisted that the second train be accepted under Regulation 5. This made little or no sense. The second train was slightly *less* likely to find the traps at the far end of the loop set against it than the one accepted first, though the order of acceptance and the order of arrival might, of course, be different. At Glencruitten (unusually for a passing place on a single line in later years) the distant signals were worked, not fixed, so a driver would know from the distant signal being at 'on' that he would be stopping.

References to MT6 files relate to the former Board of Trade files of its Inspecting Officers (the BoT was later subsumed into the Ministry of Transport), now in the safe keeping of the National Archives, as are the RAIL files. Details of the history of Tylwch station in the 20th century will be in a future book in the Wild Swan series chronicling the history of the lines of the Cambrian Railways.

My thanks go to David Stirling of the Signalling Record Society for his ever-willing help, and advice.

Destination Shelton, Again

by CYRIL GOLDING

Following on from the success of my first 'industrial' visit to North Staffordshire, which was recalled in *BRJ* No. 55, I could not wait to make a return visit to the area. It would have to be on a weekday, in the hope of seeing more of the locomotives at work. An opportunity arose during the second week of the Bolton Wakes holiday, when on 8th July 1958, I again set out for a day in North Staffordshire. Shortly before the start of this holiday I had purchased a motor scooter which would prove more flexible than the local buses.

Having seen a shed full of interesting locomotives at Victoria Colliery during my earlier visit, I made directly for that location. Here I was rewarded by the sight of their three six-coupled saddle tanks at work, No. 11, No. 15 and No. 16.

Just after photographing them, my enthusiasm was diminished somewhat, by being caught downwind when one of them had a priming fit. It was only after a visit to their pithead baths that I was able to leave Victoria and continue with my quest, by moving on to Norton Colliery.

Before vesting day, Norton had been part of the same colliery group as Victoria, and therefore was another place to have Robert Heath style locomotives. Here my plan of seeing working locomotives went a little astray, as although a weekday, little or no activity was to be found. All was not lost, however, as I managed to find some staff and I was soon being shown into the locomotive shed. This contained three locomotives, two steam and a diesel. The steam were

small Robert Heath four-coupled saddle tanks similar to No. 7 photographed on my first visit to Victoria, but not disfigured by large spark arresters on their chimneys.

As before, they conformed to a standard outline. At the time I had to assume that one, No. 10, had started out as a normal-looking Manning, Wardle product. But from information given in *Industrial Locomotives of North Staffordshire*, one of the Handbooks published by the Industrial Railway Society in 1997, this was disproved. No. 10 is credited as being built by Heath.

Perceiving my disappointment that nothing was working and that I had, in their view, wobbled all the way from Bolton (the 'L' plates displayed on my new scooter having been the subject of

Victoria Colliery No. 11, black Hawthorn 949/88, one of the three externally similar six-coupled locomotives seen at work in the colliery yard. The spark arrester detracted from an otherwise pleasing design. I cannot recall if this was the culprit that covered me in wet soot!

some wry banter), it was agreed to start up the diesel, *Norton No. 2*. A few minutes later, the six-coupled Bagnall had both steam locomotives standing in the sunlight, ready for me to take some photographs.

I have now long forgotten the actual reason why Norton Colliery was inactive. Indeed in my first draft of this account, I had written that the colliery was on holiday. Then I was enlightened by a neighbour, who pointed out the strength of the Potters' holiday in relation to all the North Staffordshire collieries. This led me to make enquiries of friends who lived in the district about that time and to contact one of the local newspapers. I have now established that the men at Norton still had just over three weeks of

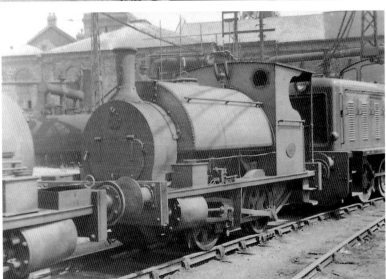

Top left: *Norton Colliery No. 6, one of the two steam locomotives pulled out of the shed for a photograph. Note the fleet number carried on the front of the chimney.*

Norton Colliery No. 10.

Norton Colliery No. 2. Over the years, Bagnall provided a number of their diesel locomotives to the area. It was spotless when photographed with the two steamers in tow.

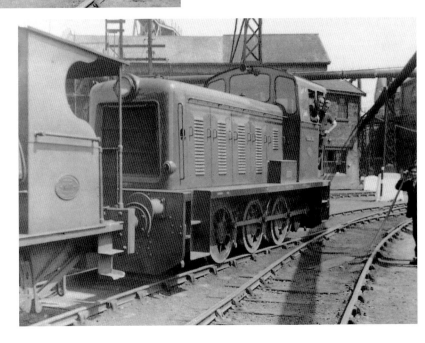

work before the start of their summer shutdown. That said, just to add to the mystery, I now find, from details in the above-mentioned Handbook, that Norton should have had a second diesel locomotive, *Norton No. 1*, at the time of my visit.

On leaving Norton, I made my way towards the city centre, Handley, and then onto the side of the railway crossing at Shelton Iron & Steel. The arrangements put in hand during my earlier visit paid dividends and I was led this time to a different section of the complex, in order that I could find more of the fleet. One of the first locomotives to come into view was *Hawarden*, a fine-looking Bagnall. This, a wartime addition to the fleet, was a very substantial four-coupled saddle tank. I was also able to photograph another of their large six-coupled Hudswell, Clarke side tanks, *Peplow*, this being one of two in the fleet with a downward slope to the front section of their tank tops. Moving on, we found *Progress*, another six-coupled locomotive, a saddle tank built by Hawthorn, Leslie. I had still not seen their Dubs crane tank, which proved to be somewhat nomadic, but it was eventually tracked down and photographed.

Shelton's Hawarden, *a large four-wheeled machine. Just look at that chimney!*

Shelton's Peplow, *one of two. I did not think they had the style of the earlier* Myreside.

Shelton's Dübs 4101/01. *This took some tracking down, but at last I had a photograph of a Dübs crane tank.*

Shelton's Progress *appears to be dwarfed by the old boiler being used as a water tank.*

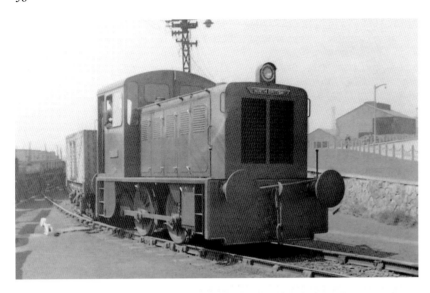

Shelton's Panther. *Shelton received a number of these NBL diesel hydraulic locomotives before moving onto diesel electric types.*

Holditch Colliery Sentinel 9534/52. The NCB purchased a number of 100hp and 200hp Sentinel locomotives. This is one of the 100hp size, photographed just prior to my footplate trip.

Parkhouse Colliery Daisy. *Larger Peckett designs went somewhat over the top at times, but this six-coupled locomotive was very neat.*

Regrettably, all good things had to come to an end, as it was time to start my journey back north. Again I was able to leave Shelton well pleased with what I had seen and, as before, promised to return. On the down side, however, another new North British diesel hydraulic locomotive, *Panther*, had been added to the fleet. A short time later, the headgear at Holditch Colliery came into view. The working locomotive here was a Sentinel, whose driver gave me a footplate trip to the shed. This contained *Winwick*, a large six-coupled Hudswell, Clarke side tank. The ride on the Sentinel was my second in two days, the first at Warrington Gas Works.

Back on the A34 road, I was soon side-tracked again, when I saw a locomotive still working at the Parkhouse Colliery. This proved to be *Daisy*, a neat six-coupled Peckett saddle tank, which I just had time to photograph before it slipped into the locomotive shed. This already contained two more Pecketts, but these were both smaller four-coupled machines; the 1904 example appeared to be helping to prop up part of the shed roof.

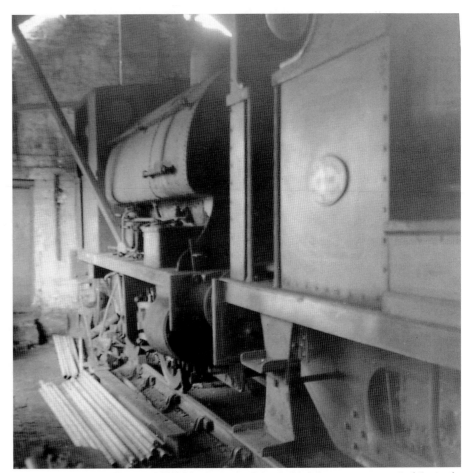

Parkhouse Colliery's Peckett 973/04 in the back of the shed helping to prop up part of the roof.

REWLEY ROAD

Mr. D. Horne sent in these lovely pictures of the swing bridge over the canal linking the Oxford Canal with the River Thames on the approach to Oxford Rewley Road as a follow-up to the article in BRJ No. 73. He says he took them in February 1954. The first one shows staff opening the bridge to allow narrow boats through. Note the red flag held from the signal box window and 2P 40411 interrupted from shunting in the LMR goods yard. In the right background a 'Hall' can just be seen removing stock from the up bay in the WR station. Note the separate girder bridge carrying point rodding and signal wires clear of the swing bridge.

This view shows the bridge swung open for the boats to pass from the main River Thames into the Oxford Canal. In the background 1425 was arriving in the WR station with a lunchtime through autocoach from Blenheim & Woodstock. The WR Oxford North signal box is seen on the right.

AN 'UPLIFTING' INCIDENT

by DEREK MUTTON

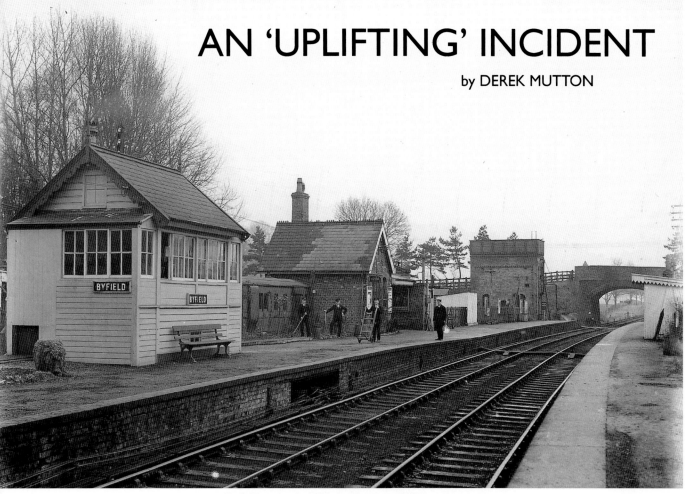

Byfield station in 1938, looking towards Towcester.

Gazing out of my window on this cold February day, watching the snow falling, the wind whipping it into little drifts in the garden, I was suddenly reminded of another February, more than sixty years ago, when after a relatively mild spell the land was plunged into a white frozen hell that seemed to go on and on with very little let-up for a month or more.

I was, of course, thinking of the winter of 1947, when it was so cold that icicles formed on the underside of engine cab roofs as steam glands leaked, and grew longer until the vibration snapped then off. Water columns froze, and even coal in tenders which had been watered froze into almost unmanageable lumps. It was during this hard spell of weather that I had the experience of being trapped in a snowdrift overnight, as mentioned in the book *Off Northampton Shed*.

However, to my own knowledge, it was not a completely isolated incident during that winter, as, not more than half a dozen

miles away during that cold spell, but on a different branch line, another very similar incident occurred, although with a more spectacular outcome.

Although neither I, nor any other Northampton locoman was involved, the 'news' of the incident was learned, by anyone willing to listen, via 'Robbo' Robson (or was it Robinson?), a veteran Blisworth driver, who related the tale whilst quaffing a pint (or two) in the 'snug' of the Blisworth Station Hotel several days after the incident, where several of us locomen were gathered during our refreshment break from shunting duties, etc, whilst marshalling trains within the two yards (sidings really) at Blisworth.

Apparently it was again an evening local pick-up goods train that was involved. This one was travelling from Broom Junction along the SMJ towards Blisworth, engine crews having exchanged trains at Stratford-upon-Avon, as was normal, and from where, after a shunting and refreshment

period, they were now heading home-wards. The next port of call was to have been Woodford Halse sidings – on the LNER (ex Great Central Railway) – where an exchange of a few wagons would be normal.

However, as the train began to trundle through Byfield Station (travelling slowly after the exchange of the single-line 'staff' adjacent to the signal box at the west end of the station), it ran into an enormous drift of snow which brought the train to a crunching stop.

The driver, it was said, reversed the train and attempted to charge the drift, but even after uncoupling the engine from the few wagons they had behind the tender and so gaining a little more momentum, little impression on the packed snow was made. In fact, after about the fourth attempt the engine had impacted the snow so much that the front of the engine was lifted off the rails, causing the top of the chimney to jam under the brickwork of the over-bridge

Byfield station, looking west towards Broom Junction in 1948.

Byfield station building.

R. C. RILEY, CTY. TRANSPORT TREASURY

No. 3520 with a westbound train but no headcode, alongside the platform at Byfield on 20th July 1946.   H. C. CASSERLEY

at the eastern end of the station! And this, if my memory of the engine is correct, was with one of the later and heavier Johnson Class 3 freight engines.

The drift had obviously been created by the wind funnelling the ever-worsening snow storm through the space between the brickwork supporting the water tank and that of the bridge approach itself, and on to the line at the end of the station platforms, and thus right up to the bridge. My memory is somewhat hazy after all these years, and I cannot find any notes I may have made after hearing the tale, but I believe the engine was 3767, a Johnson Midland 0–6–0, and a Stratford-on-Avon engine. The fireman was, again I believe, Frank Whitmore of Blisworth, but I have no recollection of who the driver was, even if his name was mentioned, being more interested in a fireman colleague, although the driver, too, was very likely to have been stationed at Blisworth.

Although the train (reportedly of only five wagons and a brake) had come to a somewhat unexpected and sudden stop, there were no serious injuries to either footplate crew or the guard, and they, like myself and Ernie during the night of our incident at Wappenham, had to spend the night in somewhat unusual surroundings, although theirs was perhaps more congenial as it was spent in the company of the signalman in his box, until he went home at 10pm (when traffic on the branch would normally cease for the night). Rumour had it that they were then offered accommodation at the home of the station master,

Byfield signal box.

but that was probably old Robbo just embellishing his story.

More likely the train crew were then left to their own devices to await either rescue via road or rail. Neither was forthcoming until the next morning, so they were forced to spend a not too uncomfortable night, no doubt in the relative comfort of the signal cabin.

When rescue did come the next day, and the snow cleared from around the engine, the train was pulled backwards a couple of yards or so, and very luckily the engine dropped back on the rails. The damage to the engine appeared to be fairly minor, two broken studs at the base of the chimney, and the bridge was little the worse for wear, there being only a double groove or scratch on the brickwork of the underside of the arch above the up line. However, although soon blackened by smoke, the mark was

easily discernible for some time afterwards. Again, according to Robbo, it took the platelayers more than a little time not only to clear the drift, but also to chip away what had become solid blocks of ice where the leading wheels had been suspended.

Sadly, that railway, like the Banbury branch, has been gone for forty years and more, but I wonder if the bridge is still there, and if the scratch can still be seen.

Such incidents were, I am sure, not uncommon during the chaos of that snowbound couple of months and, of course, when the thaw came, flooding created its own hazards, with many branch line cuttings flooded to a depth which necessitated slow progress through the water with dampers closed in order that water being forced into the ashpan did not extinguish the fire.

Metropolitan 'A' class No. 41, regularly outstationed at Brill, is seen here at Quainton Road with two wagons of coal and the regular branch carriage prior to departure to Brill in August 1935.

LONDON TRANSPORT

FORGOTTEN JOURNEY
QUAINTON ROAD TO WOTTON

by PAUL KARAU

On 30th November 2010 it will be 75 years since the last train crossed the Buckinghamshire pastures from Brill to Quainton Road along the Duke of Buckingham's tramway. Yet that quiet railway backwater is still held with affection by railway students born long after its disappearance. Perhaps the appeal of the rustic tramway is heightened by being included and mapped as such an unlikely outpost of the London Transport system, resulting in the sight of a London Transport liveried 'A' class 4–4–0T weaving its way through trees and hedges with a single coach and a couple of wagons. Another factor is surely the romantic allure of a single beckoning track crossing the road and heading off across the fields.

Various photos of the line have accompanied accounts over the years, but the primary object of this feature is to illustrate as much of the route as material allows in order to provide a long overdue pictorial record.

It was certainly not our intention to add to the number of previous historical accounts, but instead to offer the briefest outline of events as a useful reference.

Following the failure of the Buckinghamshire Railway to proceed with its southern extension from Claydon to Aylesbury, a new company, the Aylesbury and Buckingham Railway, was incorporated in 1860 to build a similar link from the recently constructed Buckinghamshire Railway, leased to the LNWR, to Aylesbury.

The Marquis of Chandos, then chairman of the L&NWR and later to become the third Duke of Buckingham, made it clear that if the line was routed to the west of Quainton Hill and south-west of Quainton village, he would become chairman and provide financial investment. His offer was accepted and landowner Sir Harry Verney joined forces as deputy chairman.

The new station where the A&BR joined the Buckinghamshire Railway near Claydon was named Verney Junction after Sir Harry, and when the line opened to Aylesbury in 1868, intermediate stations were provided at Winslow Road, Granborough Road and Quainton Road. Waddesdon was a later addition in 1897.

Following the completion, the Duke of Buckingham turned his attention to the deferred Wotton Tramway intended to link his estate and family home at Wotton House to the new line at Quainton Road.

The line was built privately, mostly on land owned by the Duke, a small portion near Quainton Road being leased. With minimal works, construction began in September 1870 using local workers and was completed to Wotton the following April. At the request of the local people, the line was continued on to Brill and opened in the summer of 1872.

In 1894, five years after the death of the third Duke of Buckingham, the working of the line was taken over by the Oxford and Aylesbury Tramroad Co. which had been established in 1888 as part of a scheme to build a line from Oxford to connect with the tramway at Brill. Not long after taking control, the O&AT improved the line by replacing the bridge rail and longitudinal sleepers of the old baulk road with flat-bottomed rail spiked to transverse sleepers.

In the meantime, the Aylesbury & Buckingham Railway had been absorbed by the Metropolitan Railway in 1890 and a new line opened from Rickmansworth to Aylesbury in 1892, providing direct services to Baker Street.

In 1899 the Metropolitan Railway took over the working of the Brill Tramway and the rail-level platforms were rebuilt to the standard 3ft height to suit a Metropolitan coach provided for services. Later, in 1903, the track at Brill was in a bad state, so the whole station was relaid with more substantial bullhead rail. Derailments along the line were far too frequent, so the rest of the line was subsequently relaid in part worn bullhead and replacement sleepers.

The new Great Central line from Marylebone to the North used the Metropolitan Railway between Harrow South Junction and Quainton Road, so the whole of the line from Harrow South Junction to Verney Junction fell under the control of the newly formed Metropolitan and Great Central Joint Committee which from 1906 was also responsible for the Brill Tramway.

Ironically, with the tramway having been significantly improved, it might have suddenly seemed a rather quaint option in the face of arriving main-line competition.

The Great Western and Great Central Joint Committee of 1899 built a new line from Princes Risborough to Grendon Underwood Junction on the GC line some three miles north of Quainton Road. This bridged the Brill Tramway at Wotton and, when opened in 1905, offered the locality a main-line service from a new station nearby.

Then as part of the Great Western's desire for a shorter and more competitive route between Paddington and Birmingham, the company built a new line from the new GW & GC Joint at Ashendon Junction to Aynho Junction, passing beneath the Brill Tramway at Wood Siding. Opening in 1910, the GWR offered the inhabitants of Brill a main-line service from a station named Brill and Ludgershall. The only consolation was that even at some three-quarters of a mile from the village, the tramway terminus was considerably nearer than the new station.

In 1911, application was made to the Board of Trade to increase the maximum speed over the tramway from 12 mph to 25 mph and, following an inspection, this was granted, reducing the journey time to 32 minutes. It was also around that time that Metropolitan 'A' class 4–4–0Ts were first used on the tramway, in particular Nos. 23 and 41 which, as things turned out, worked the line until closure. They alternated each week, the fresh one being despatched from Neasden each Monday and shedded at Brill through to the following Monday morning. The timetable provided for four return trips each day (except Sundays) and an extra train on Saturday evenings, and goods traffic was conveyed with the single coach as a mixed formation.

396
8·492

Probably No. 41 again, this time smokebox towards Brill and gently approaching Quainton level crossing with another mixed train. From Quainton Road the line ran alongside the Quainton to Akeman Street road, separated only by a neatly clipped hedge all the way to Waddesdon.
S. H. FREESE

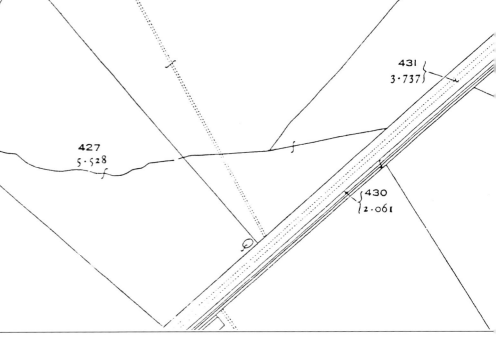

431
3·737

427
5·528

430
2·061

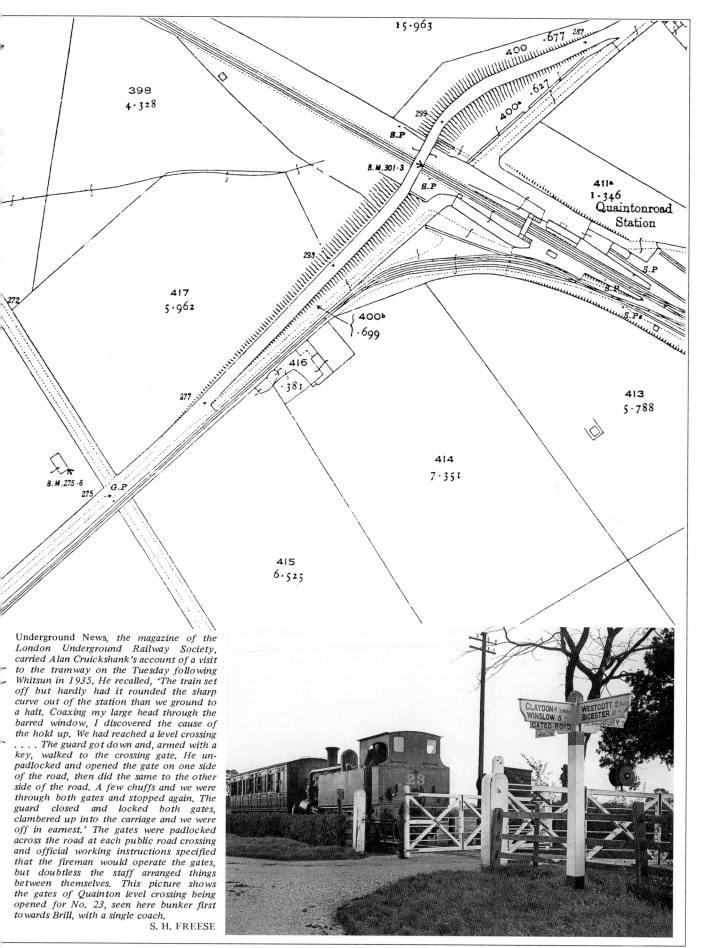

15·963

398
4·3²⁸

400 ·677 287

299 ·627

400ᵃ

S.P

B.M.301·3

S.P

411ᵃ
1·346
Quaintonroad
Station

293

S.P

272

S.P

417
5·962

400ᵇ
·699

416

S.B.

S.P

277

381

413
5·788

414
7·35¹

B.M.275·6

G.P

275

415
6·525

Underground News, *the magazine of the London Underground Railway Society, carried Alan Cruickshank's account of a visit to the tramway on the Tuesday following Whitsun in 1935. He recalled, 'The train set off but hardly had it rounded the sharp curve out of the station than we ground to a halt. Coaxing my large head through the barred window, I discovered the cause of the hold up. We had reached a level crossing . . . . The guard got down and, armed with a key, walked to the crossing gate. He un-padlocked and opened the gate on one side of the road, then did the same to the other side of the road. A few chuffs and we were through both gates and stopped again. The guard closed and locked both gates, clambered up into the carriage and we were off in earnest.' The gates were padlocked across the road at each public road crossing and official working instructions specified that the fireman would operate the gates, but doubtless the staff arranged things between themselves. This picture shows the gates of Quainton level crossing being opened for No. 23, seen here bunker first towards Brill, with a single coach.*

S. H. FREESE

All maps taken from Ordnance Survey for 1920. Crown copyright reserved.

Further along the Quainton straight road, looking back towards Quainton level crossing in 1935. The road was running parallel on the left the other side of the hedge. The apparent change in gradient seems to have marked the foot of the 1 in 78 climb away from the crossing. We have so far failed to locate a gradient profile of the line, which may explain such absence from previous accounts. The Board of Trade inspection of 1894 records the radii of the sharper curves and provides a list of the steeper gradients but without location. The line followed the gently undulating land surface and, as far as we can establish, this picture may have been taken from near the summit of that first gradient. If that is the case, then there was an equivalent 1 in 78 descent behind the photographer towards Waddesdon Road. These gradients were sufficient to warrant mention in official working instructions about descending inclines, 'especially those on the Quainton straight road, at Blue Bottle and between Brill and Wotton . . . sufficient power must be put down by the Guard in the Train to keep the Train back from pressing on the engine, the engine brake being reserved for any emergency.' After this minor summit, the line was on a steady descent all the way through to Wotton, which is said to have been 50ft below Quainton Road, although Ordnance Survey spot heights on the adjacent roads seem to indicate a 31ft difference. From Wotton there was a steady climb all the way to Brill. Incidentally, the road was on the other side of the left-hand hedge.
LONDON TRANSPORT

The approach to Waddesdon Road station, just less than 1¼ miles from Quainton Road, in 1935, showing the entrance to the single goods siding diverging behind the platform. The yard entry points were locked by a key on the train staff; the lever is seen on the left, just beyond the loading gauge. With facing points at Waddesdon Road, Westcott and Wotton, tow roping was used to put wagons into the sidings off trains from Quainton Road. The train would stop short of the points and the leading wagon(s) for delivery would be uncoupled from the rest of the train and hooked up to the engine using the rope or chain carried on the running plate. The engine would then move forward clear of the point blades, which were afterwards changed for the siding so the wagon(s) would be towed in by the engine on the adjacent line. Wagons for collection were doubtless shunted out conventionally on the return journey, when adding them to the train gave passengers in the coach at the rear of the formation uncomfortable jolts. The buildings in the distance belonged to Hall Farm on the opposite side of the main road. The village of Waddesdon was a mile away to the east.
L&GRP

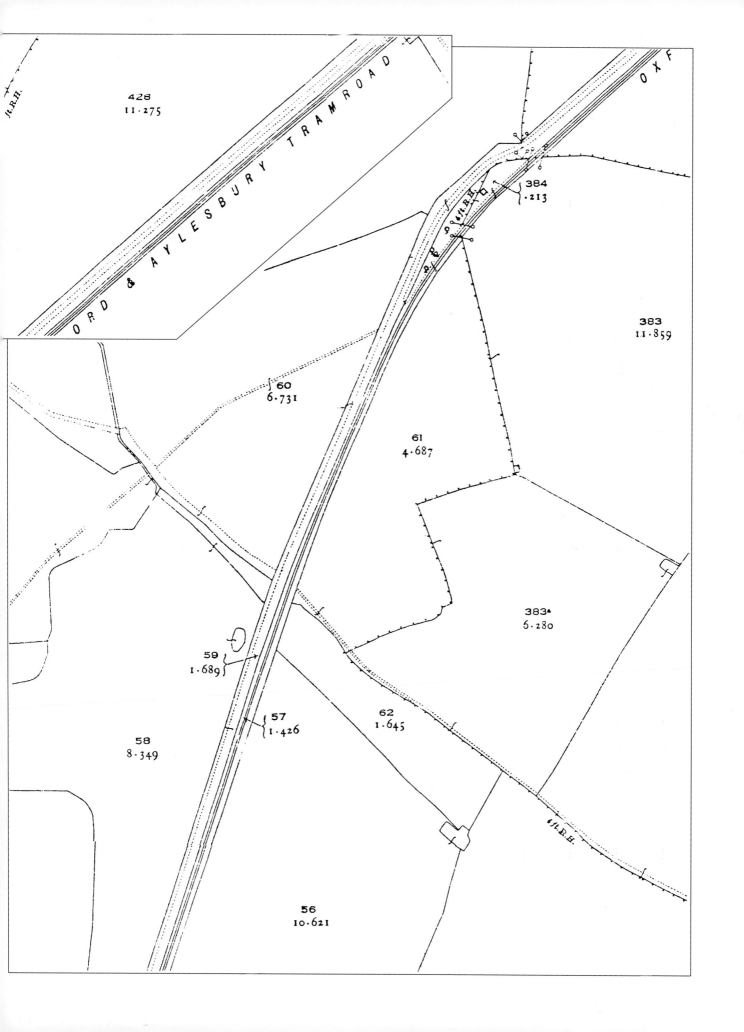

This 1935 picture of Waddesdon Road station shows the 'T' junction of the road from Quainton on the left, with the A41, the old Roman Akeman Street, and the overlapping north side crossing gates. The 1936 sale list gives the dimensions of the booking office and waiting room as 24ft x 10ft 9in, and the goods shed, to the right, as 12ft x 9ft. The platform was given as 37 yds x 2 yds. LONDON TRANSPORT

The station buildings on the line were built to serve the original rail-level platforms, so when the platforms were raised to the standard height of 3ft, a low-level portion had to be retained. The loading platform beyond was 9ft x 6ft. According to an 1890s staff list, a clerk in charge, an auditor and a gatekeeper were based at this remote location. On the other side of the level crossing, the line left the roadside and headed off across the fields. S. W. BAKER

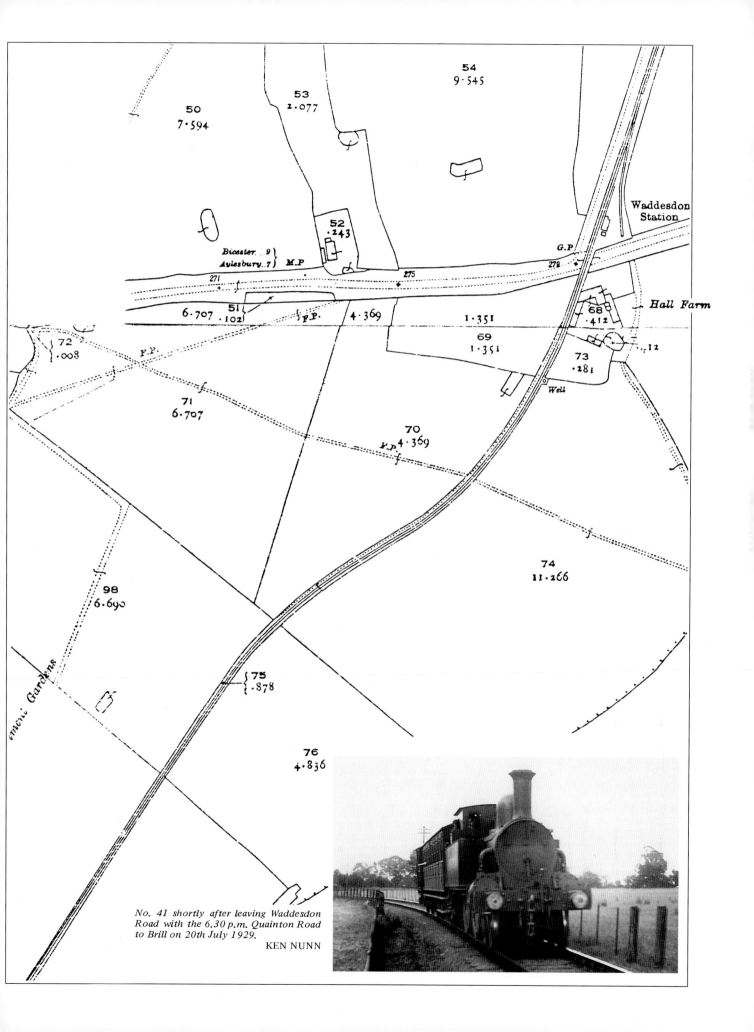

54
9·545

53
2·077

50
7·594

52
·243

Bicester 9 }
Aylesbury 7 } M.P

271

275

279   G.P

Waddesdon Station

Hall Farm

51
6·707 ·102

F.P.

4·369

1·351

69
1·351

68
·412

12

73
·281

72
·008

F.P.

71
6·707

70
F.P. 4·369

Well

74
11·266

98
6·690

75
·878

76
4·836

No. 41 shortly after leaving Waddesdon Road with the 6.30 p.m. Quainton Road to Brill on 20th July 1929.

KEN NUNN

The tramway's hedge-lined approach from across the fields, as seen looking north-east from the platform at Westcott in August 1935. The empty trackbed on the right was the point of divergence of the long siding which struck off south to serve the shortlived Westcott gas works. Once again the throat of the sidings, 1¾ miles from Quainton Road, was provided with a loading gauge.
LONDON TRANSPORT

Looking in the opposite direction on the same occasion, with the tramway workers' cottages on the left, and on the right, behind the platform, a glimpse of the goods yard and the yard entrance gate. The buildings on the opposite side of the road in the right background belonged to Westcott Farm and the village was just off to the right.
LONDON TRANSPORT

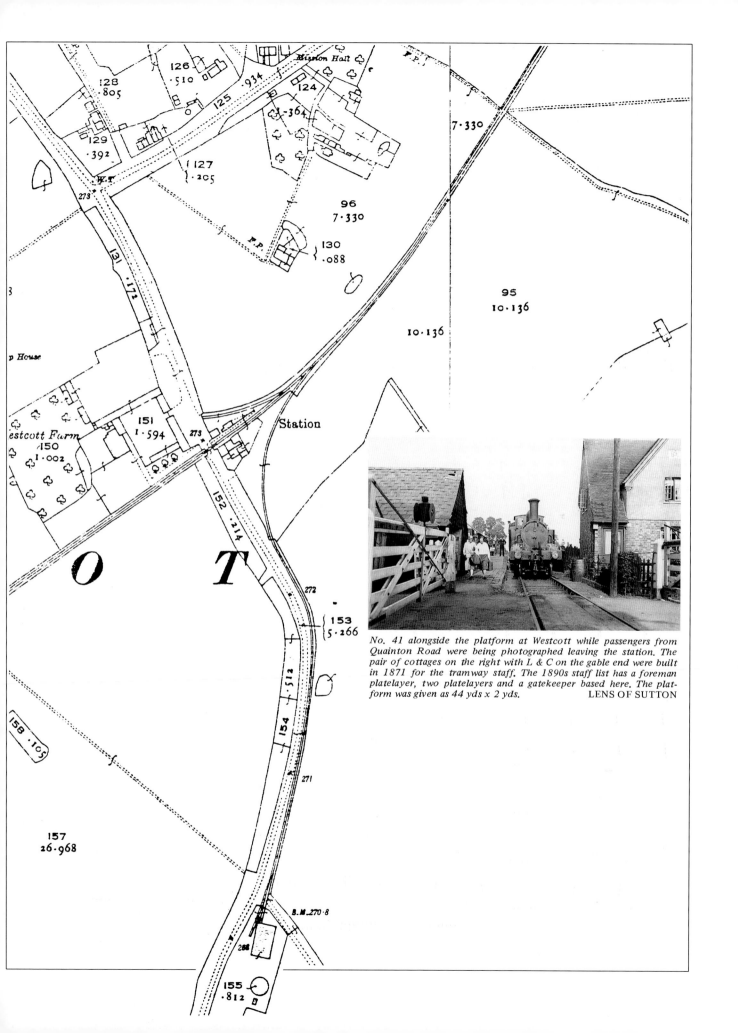

No. 41 alongside the platform at Westcott while passengers from Quainton Road were being photographed leaving the station. The pair of cottages on the right with L & C on the gable end were built in 1871 for the tramway staff. The 1890s staff list has a foreman platelayer, two platelayers and a gatekeeper based here. The platform was given as 44 yds x 2 yds.   LENS OF SUTTON

This picture was taken to the west of Westcott station, with the crossing gates prominent in the distance. The line was still on a gentle downgrade to Wotton.
C. L. TURNER

Before we leave Westcott, this February 1934 view from the edge of Westcott Farm shows the station building in the background and the 6 yd x 7 yd goods shed to the right of the entrance gate. The pair of staff cottages can be seen beyond the level crossing.
LONDON TRANSPORT

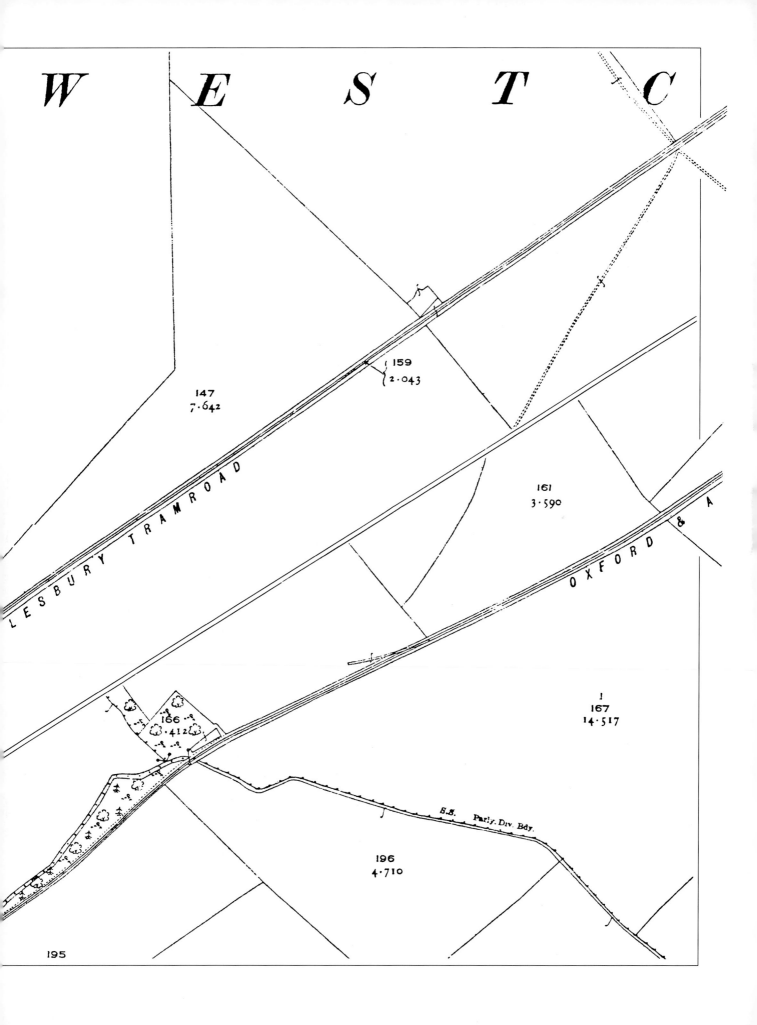

W   E   S   T   C

147
7·642

159
2·043

LESBURY TRAMROAD

161
3·590

OXFORD & A

1
167
14·517

166
·412

S.S.   Parly. Div. Bdy.

196
4·710

195

This gentle country scene was taken between Westcott and Wotton, looking back towards Quainton Road.   C. L. TURNER

225
30·499

231
·694

230
·115

C.S.   DJ.

P.B.   AYLESBURY TRAMROAD

OXFOR   179
            1·669

229
·410

177
·021   Tk.S.

228
·037

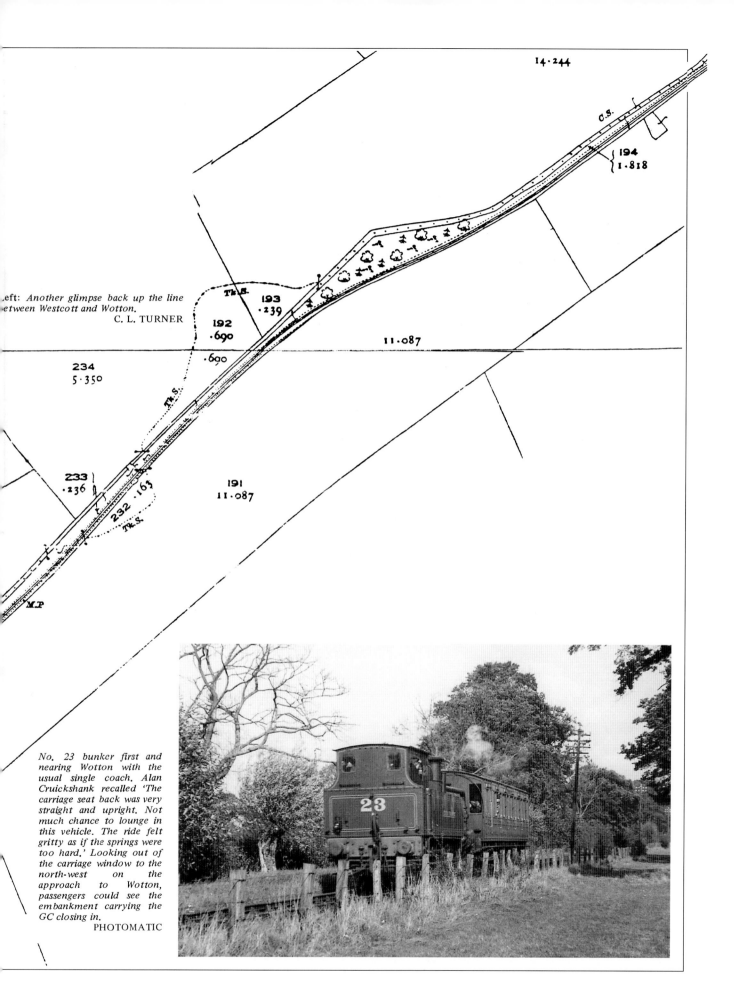

14·244

C.S.

194
1·818

Left: Another glimpse back up the line between Westcott and Wotton.
C. L. TURNER

Tk.S.

193
·239

192
·690

·690

11·087

234
5·350

Tk.S.

233
·236

232 ·16

Tk.S.

191
11·087

M.P

No. 23 bunker first and nearing Wotton with the usual single coach. Alan Cruickshank recalled 'The carriage seat back was very straight and upright. Not much chance to lounge in this vehicle. The ride felt gritty as if the springs were too hard.' Looking out of the carriage window to the north-west on the approach to Wotton, passengers could see the embankment carrying the GC closing in.
PHOTOMATIC

The Great Central link from Princes Risborough to the junction at Grendon Underwood was carried over the Brill Tramway by this 53ft span plate girder bridge, which overshadowed the curving entry of the line through Wotton station. This view was taken looking west, with the running line on the left and the goods shed siding on the right.

C. L. TURNER

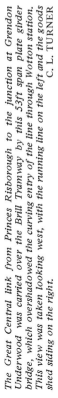
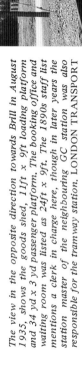

The view in the opposite direction towards Brill in August 1935, shows the goods shed, 11ft x 9ft loading platform and 34 yd x 3 yd passenger platform. The booking office and waiting room was listed as 24ft x 9ft. The 1890s staff list mentions a clerk in charge here, though in later years the station master of the neighbouring GC station was also responsible for the tramway station. LONDON TRANSPORT

No. 41 alongside the platform with more passengers leaving the train from Quainton Road. Wotton station was approximately 3¾ miles from the start of the journey.

LENS OF SUTTON

We will set out from Wotton for the remainder of the journey in the next issue, but, for now, here is a glimpse of the line heading away from Wotton towards Brill on a north-west heading through Navigation Spinney on 6th October 1935.   S. W. BAKER